HARRAP'S

Arabic phrasebook

Samer Abboud
Mahmoud Fathi El-Kastawy

Mc
Graw
Hill

New York Chicago San Francisco Lisbon London Madrid Mexico City
Milan New Delhi San Juan Seoul Singapore Sydney Toronto

ISBN-10: 0-07-148626-7
ISBN-13: 978-0-07-148626-2

Editor & Project Manager
Anna Stevenson

Prepress
Nicolas Echallier

CONTENTS

INTRODUCTION

This brand new English-Arabic phrasebook from Harrap is ideal for anyone wishing to try out their foreign language skills while travelling abroad. The information is practical and clearly presented, helping you to overcome the language barrier and mix with the locals.

Each section features a list of useful words and a selection of common phrases: some of these you will read or hear, while others will help you to express yourself. The simple phonetic transcription system, specifically designed for English speakers, ensures that you will always make yourself understood.

The book also includes a mini bilingual dictionary of around 2,000 words, so that more adventurous users can build on the basic structures and engage in more complex conversations.

Concise information on local culture and customs is provided, along with practical tips to save you time. After all, you're on holiday – time to relax and enjoy yourself! There is also a food and drink glossary to help you make sense of menus, and ensure that you don't miss out on any of the national or regional specialities.

Remember that any effort you make will be appreciated. So don't be shy – have a go!

ABBREVIATIONS USED IN THIS BOOK

adj	adjective	*n*	neuter
adv	adverb	*pl*	plural
f	feminine	*sing*	singular
m	masculine	*v*	verb

PRONUNCIATION

Alphabet

Unlike English, Arabic is written from right to left so be aware when reading signs or when trying to make out the letters in a particular word or phrase. Each of the letters in the Arabic alphabet has a basic form but is modified in shape according to its position in a word, depending on whether it appears alone, at the beginning, in the middle or at the end of a word. A number of letters share the same shape and are only distinguished by dots above the letters (known as diacritic dots).

The following table shows how each letter looks like either alone, or in the beginning, middle or end of a word.

alone	beginning	middle	end	transliteration
ا	ا	ا	ا	a/aa
ب	بـ	ـبـ	ـب	b
ت	تـ	ـتـ	ـت	t
ث	ثـ	ـثـ	ـث	th
ج	جـ	ـجـ	ـج	j
ح	حـ	ـحـ	ـح	H
خ	خـ	ـخـ	ـخ	kh
د	د	ـد	ـد	d
ذ	ذ	ـذ	ـذ	dh
ر	ر	ـر	ـر	r
ز	ز	ـز	ـز	z
س	سـ	ـسـ	ـس	s
ش	شـ	ـشـ	ـش	sh
ص	صـ	ـصـ	ـص	S
ض	ضـ	ـضـ	ـض	D
ط	طـ	ـطـ	ـط	T

ظ	ظ	ظ	ظ	Z
ع	ع	ع	ع	A
غ	غ	غ	غ	gh
ف	ف	ف	ف	f
ق	ق	ق	ق	q
ك	ك	ك	ك	k
ل	ل	ل	ل	l
م	م	م	م	m
ن	ن	ن	ن	n
ه	ه	ه	ه	h
و	و	و	و	w/oo/ow
ي	ي	ي	ي	y/ee/ay/ey
ء	ء	ء	ء	'

Pronunciation

Every phrase given in Arabic in this guide is followed by its pronunciation shown in italics. If you follow the phonetic transcription you will be able to make yourself understood in Arabic. Note that when a translation differs according to whether it refers to a masculine or feminine form (for example, if you are addressing a man or a woman) this is shown in the transcription; with the masculine form first and separated from the feminine by a slash, eg:

how do you do!

كيف حالك!

kayfa Haa-lak/kayfa Haa-lik!

The following pronunciations of Arabic letters are similar to English sounds:

letter	name of letter	transcription	pronunciation
ا	*alif*	*a*	as in c**a**r
ب	*ba*	*b*	as in **b**ig
ت	*ta*	*t*	as in **t**eam
ث	*tha*	*th*	as in **th**ree
ج	*jim*	*j*	as in **j**ar

خ	kha	kh	as in Scottish English lo**ch**
د	dal	d	as in **d**oor
ذ	dhal	dh	as in **th**e
ر	ra	r	as in **r**ound
ز	zay	z	as in **z**ebra
س	sin	s	as in **s**uper
ش	shin	sh	as in **sh**oot
ف	fa	f	as in **f**ar
ك	kaf	k	as in **k**ey
ل	lam	l	as in **l**ive
م	mim	m	as in **m**ajor
ن	noon	n	as in **n**ight
ه	ha	h	as in **h**ome
و	waw	oo	as in c**oo**l
ي	ya	ee	as in st**ee**r

The following sounds do not occur in English and so we have used the following codes to transcribe them:

letter	name of letter	transcription	pronunciation
ح	ha	H	similar to the **h** in **h**ot but pronounced in the back of the throat
ص	saad	S	similar to the **so** in **so**b
ض	daad	D	similar to the **do** in **do**t
ط	ta	T	similar to the **tau** in **tau**ght
ظ	za	Z	similar to the **za** in ba**za**ar
ع	ayn	A	*ayn* is probably one of the hardest letters to pronounce; try to tighten the larynx muscles so that the flow of air through the throat is partially choked off while saying something resembling the letter **a**. One way to practise is to say the word **aargh**
غ	ghayn	gh	a rolled r sound, like the French **r**, pronounced in the back of the throat

| ق | qaf | q | similar to **k** but pronounced in the back of the throat |
| ء | hamza | ' | The *hamza* is similar to the glottal stop in English, familiar as the Cockney pronunciation of the **tt** in bo**tt**le or the sound between the syllables in the exclamation **uh-oh**. |

In Arabic, short vowels (**a**, **e**, **i**, **u**) are not considered part of the alphabet but are written as marks above or below the consonant. Short vowel sounds will, however, appear in the transcription of the word and will be represented by one letter (*a, e, i, u*). The pronunciation of long vowels and diphthongs is indicated in the transcription by two letters (such as *aa, ee, oo*). Vowel sounds are pronounced as follows:

Short Vowels

a	as in h**a**d
e	as in b**e**t
i	as in h**i**t
u	as in p**u**t

Long Vowels

aa	as in b**a**d but longer
ee	as in f**ee**
oo	as in b**oo**

Diphthongs

ay	as in d**ay**
ey	as in wh**y**
ow	as in h**ow**

The Arabic translations provided in this book are taken from classical (literary) Arabic, which is the standard Arabic language. Each Arab country, however, has its own unique dialect which is used in day-to-day conversations and exists in spoken form only. All Arabic speakers will be able to understand what you are saying to them and will be able to converse with you in classical Arabic. Don't let this stop you, however, from learning words in the local dialect!

EVERYDAY CONVERSATION

Both men and women often greet each other by shaking hands and kissing each other on the cheek (sometimes twice, sometimes three times). However, this is not expected from foreign visitors and nor is it necessarily welcomed. When greeting someone of the same sex it is polite to shake their hand and offer a simple "nice to meet you" (*forSa sa-Aee-da*). If greeting someone of the opposite sex you may want to gently place your hand on your chest as a sign of respect. This avoids physical contact with the other person if they do not wish to be touched. Do not take this personally, as it could be for a personal, social or religious reason. The best thing to do is follow the cue of the person you are greeting. In more formal contexts such as a hotel or restaurant, you may want to greet someone by saying *mar-Haba* (hello) which is slightly more formal and appropriate then *ah-lan* (hi), which is how you would greet friends or close acquaintances. In the evenings it is more common to bid someone farewell by saying *maAa as-salaa-ma* (goodbye) than it is to say *tiS-bah Aala khayr* (goodnight), although it is appropriate to use either.

The basics

bye	سلام	*salaam*
excuse me	لو سمحت	*low sa-maHt*
good afternoon	نهارك سعيد	*nahaa-rak sa-Aeed*
goodbye	مع السلامة	*maAa as-salaa-ma*
good evening	مساء الخير	*masa' al-khayr*
good morning	صباح الخير	*Sa-baH al-khayr*
goodnight	تصبح على خير	*tiS-baH Aala khayr*
hello	مرحبا	*mar-Haba*
hi	أهلاً	*ah-lan*
nice to meet you	فرصة سعيدة	*forSa sa-Aee-da*
no	لا	*la*
OK	حسناً	*Hasa-nan*
pardon	معذرة	*maA-dhira*

please	من فضلك min faD-lik
thanks, thank you	شكراً shok-ran
yes	نعم na-Aam

Expressing yourself

I'd like ...
... أنا أريد
ana o-reed ...

we'd like ...
... نحن نريد
naH-noo no-reed ...

do you want ...?
هل تريد / تريدي ...؟
hal to-reed/hal to-ree-dee ...?

do you have ...?
هل لديك ...؟
hal la-day-ka/hal la-day-ke ...?

is there a ...?
هل يوجد هنا ...؟
hal yoo-jad hu-na ...?

are there any ...?
هل يوجد هنا ...؟
hal yoo-jad hu-na ...?

how?
كيف؟
keyfa?

why?
لماذا؟
li-maa-dha?

when?
متى؟
mata?

what?

ماذا؟

maa-dha?

where is...?

أين ...؟

ayna...?

where are...?

أين ...؟

ayna...?

how much is it?

كم يكلف هذا؟

kam you-kalif ha-dha?

what is it?

ماهى؟

maa he-ya?

do you speak English?

هل تتحدث إنجليزي؟

hal tata-Had-dath in-glee-zee?

where are the toilets, please?

أين الحمّام من فضلك؟

ayna al-Ham-mam min faD-lak?

how are you?

كيف حالك؟

keyfa Haa-lak/keyfa Haa-lik?

fine, thanks

بخير. شكراً

be-khayr. shok-ran

thanks very much

شكراً جزيلاً

shok-ran ja-zee-lan

no, thanks

لا. شكراً

la. shok-ran

yes, please
نعم. من فضلك
naAam, min faD-lak

you're welcome
عفواً
Aaf-wan

see you later
أراك لاحقاً
araa-ka laa-Hiqan/araa-ke laa-Hiqan

I'm sorry
أنا آسف
ana aa-sif/ana aa-sifa

Understanding

انتبه	attention!
لا ...	do not...
دخول	entrance
خروج	exit
مجاناً	free
ممنوع انتظار السيارات	no parking
ممنوع التدخين	no smoking
مفتوح	open
معطل	out of order
محجوز	reserved
حمّام	toilets

السلام عليكم
as-salamo Aalay-kum
 = greeting meaning "peace be upon you"

وعليكم السلام
wa Aalay-kum as-salam
 = reply form to the above, meaning "and on you be peace"

يوجد ...
yoo-jad ...
there's/there are ...

مرحباً
mar-Haba
welcome

هل تمانع إذا ...؟
hal to-maa-niA idha ...?
do you mind if ...?

لحظة من فضلك
laH-Za min faD-lak
one moment, please

تفضل بالجلوس
tafaD-Dal bel-joloos
please take a seat

PROBLEMS UNDERSTANDING ARABIC

Expressing yourself

pardon?
معذرة! ماذا قلت؟
maA-dhira! maa-dha qolt?

what?
ماذا؟
maa-dha?

could you repeat that, please?
ممكن تقول ذلك مرة ثانية من فضلك؟
mom-kin ta-qool dha-lik mar-ra thaa-ne-ya min faD-lak?

could you speak more slowly?
ممكن تتكلم ببطء أكثر؟
mom-kin tit-kal-lim bi-boT' ak-thar?

I don't understand
لا أفهم ذلك
la af-ham dha-lik

I understand a little Arabic
أفهم قليلا من اللغة العربية
af-ham qa-lee-lan min al-logha al-Aara-bay-ya

I can understand Arabic but I can't speak it
أفهم اللغة العربية ولكن لا أخدثها
af-ham al-logha al-Aara-bay-ya wa-laa-kin la ata-Had-dath-ha

I hardly speak any Arabic
أخدث اللغة العربية بصعوبة
ata-Had-dath al-logha al-Aara-bay-ya be-Sa-Aoo-ba

do you speak English?
هل تتحدث إجليزي؟
hal tata-Had-dath in-glee-zee?

how do you say ... in Arabic
كيف تقول ... باللغة العربية؟
keyfa ta-qool ... bel-logha al-Aara-bay-ya?

how do you spell it?
كيف يمكن تهجئتها؟
keyfa yom-kin tah-ji'a-taha?

what's that called in Arabic?
كيف تسمي هذا باللغة العربية؟
keyfa to-sam-mee ha-dha bel-logha al-Aara-bay-ya?

could you write it down for me?
هل يمكن أن تكتبها لى؟
hal mom-kin an tak-tobha lee?

Understanding

هل تفهم اللغة العربية؟
hal taf-ham al-loo-gha al-Aara-bay-ya?
do you understand Arabic?

سأكتبها لك
sa ak-tobha laka/sa ak-tobha lakee
I'll write it down for you

إنها تعني ...
in-na-ha taA-nee ...
it means ...

هي عبارة عن ...
he-ya Ae-baa-ra Aan ...
it's a kind of ...

SPEAKING ABOUT THE LANGUAGE

Expressing yourself

I learned a few words from my phrasebook
تعلمت بعض الكلمات من كتيب المصطلحات
ta-Aal-lamt baAD al-kali-maat min ko-tay-yib al-mooS-Tala-Haat

I can just about get by
أنا أعرف فقط الضروري منها
ana aA-rif faqaT al-Da-roo-ree min-ha

I hardly know two words!
أنا أعرف بالكاد كلمتين
ana aA-rif bil-kaad kali-matayn

I find Arabic a difficult language
أنا أجد صعوبة في فهم اللغة العربية
ana a-jid Sa-Aoo-ba fee fahm al-logha al-Aara-bay-ya

I know the basics but no more than that
أنا أعرف فقط الأساسيات، لا أكثر
ana aA-rif faqaT al-asaa-say-yaat, la ak-thar

people speak too quickly for me
الناس يتحدثون معي بسرعة كبيرة
al-naas yata-Had-da-thoon ma-Aee be-sor-Aa ka-bee-ra

Understanding

أنت تتكلم بلكنة صحيحة
an-ta tata-kal-lam be-lak-na Sa-Hee-Ha
you have a good accent

إنك تتكلم اللغة العربية بشكل سليم
in-naka tata-kal-lam al-logh-a al-Aara-bay-ya be-shakl sa-leem
you speak very good Arabic

ASKING THE WAY

Expressing yourself

excuse me, can you tell me where the … is, please?
لو سمحت. أين أجد ...؟
low sa-maHt. ayna ajid …?

which way is it to …?
أين الطريق إلى ...؟
ayna Ta-reeq ila…

can you tell me how to get to …?
ممكن تدلني كيف أصل إلى ...؟
mom-kin ta-dol-lanee keyfa aSil ila …?

is there a … near here?
هل يوجد ... بالقرب من هنا؟
hal yoo-jad …bel-qorb min hu-na?

could you show me on the map?
ممكن تبين لى ذلك على الخريطة؟
mom-kin to-bay-yen lee dha-lik Ala al-kha-ree-Ta?

is there a map of the town somewhere?
هل يوجد خريطة للمدينة؟
hal yoo-jad kha-ree-Ta lil-ma-dee-na?

is it far?
هل هى بعيدة؟
hal he-ya ba-Aee-da?

how much is the taxi?
كم أجرة التاكسي؟
kam oj-rat al-tak-see?

I'm looking for ...

... أنا أبحث عن

ana ab-Hath Aan ...

I'm lost

أنا تائه

ana ta-'ih

Understanding

اتبع

it-baA

follow

اصعد

iS-Ad

go up

استمر

es-ta-mirr

keep going

شمال

she-maal

left

يمين

ya-meen

right

إلى الأمام

ila al-amaam

straight ahead

استدر

is-ta-dir

turn

هل أتيت ماشيا؟

hal atay-ta maa-she-yan?

are you on foot?

إنها تبعد خمس دقائق بالسيارة
in-naha tab-Aod khams da-qaa-'iq bel-say-ya-ra
it's five minutes away by car

إنها الأولى / الثانية / الثالثة على اليسار
in-naha al-'oo-la/al-thaa-ne-ya/al-thaa-le-tha Aala al-she-maal
it's the first/second/third on the left

استدر يمينا عند الدوّار
is-ta-dir ya-mee-nan Aen-da al-dow-waar
turn right at the roundabout

استدر يسارا عند البنك
is-ta-dir she-maa-lan Aen-da al-bank
turn left at the bank

الزم المخرج القادم
il-zam al-makh-raj al-qaa-dim
take the next exit

ليست بعيدة
lay-sat ba-Aee-da
it's not far

إنها قريبة جدًا من هنا
in-naha qa-ree-ba jid-dan min hu-na
it's just round the corner

GETTING TO KNOW PEOPLE

Egyptians are famous throughout the Arab world for being friendly and good-humoured. Conversations, even of a formal nature, will begin with enquiries into each other's health and that of family members before getting down to business. In informal conversation, there are many set responses which vary depending on the gender and number of people involved. You may hear various responses when you ask someone *keyfa Haa-lak* (how are you?), including *al-Hamdulil-laah*, *ana ko-way-yes* and *be-kheir* (all meaning "I am fine").

Conversation topics naturally differ from country to country, but don't be afraid to ask people you have met questions about the city or country you are visiting. Most people are friendly and willing to discuss your experiences with you.

The basics

bad	سيّئ *say-yi'*
beautiful	جميل *ja-meel*
boring	مُمِل *mo-mill*
cheap	رخيص *ra-kheeS*
expensive	غالي *ghaa-lee*
good	جيد *jayy-yid*
great	عظيم *Aa-Zeem*
interesting	مشوّق *mo-show-wiq*
nice	لطيف *la-Teef*
not bad	ليس سيّئ *lay-sa say-yi'*
well	ممتاز *mom-taaz*
to hate	يَكره *yak-rah*
to like	يُحب *yo-Hibb*
to love	يُحب *yo-Hibb*

INTRODUCING YOURSELF AND FINDING OUT ABOUT OTHER PEOPLE

Expressing yourself

my name's ...

إسمى ...
is-mee ...

what's your name?

ماإسمك؟
maa is-mak/maa is-mik?

how do you do!

كيف حالك!
keyfa Haa-lak/keyfa Haa-lik!

pleased to meet you!

فرصة سعيدة
forSa sa-Aee-da

this is my husband

هذا زوجى
ha-dha zaw-jee

this is my partner, Karen

هذه رفيقتى كارين
ha-dhe-he ra-fee-qatee ka-rin

I'm English

أنا إجليزى
ana in-glee-zee

we're Welsh

نحن من بلاد الغال
naH-noo min bilad-al Ral

I'm from ...

أنا من ...
ana min ...

where are you from?

من أين أنت؟
min ayna an-ta/min ayna an-te?

how old are you?

كم عمرك؟

kam Aom-rak/kam Aom-rik?

I'm 22

عمري اثنان وعشرون عام

Aom-ree ith-naan wa Aosh-roon Aaam

what do you do for a living?

ماذا تعمل؟

ma-dha taA-mal?

are you a student?

هل انتَ طالب / أنتِ طالبة؟

hal anta Taa-lib?/hal an-te Taa-liba?

I work

أنا أعمل

ana aA-mal

I'm studying law

أنا أدرس القانون

ana ad-ros al-qaa-noon

I'm a teacher

أنا مُدرِّس

ana modar-ris

I stay at home with the children

أنا أجلس فى البيت لرعاية الأطفال

ana aj-lis fee al-bayt li-reAaa-yat al-aT-faal

I work part-time

أنا أعمل بعض الوقت

ana aA-mal baAD al-waqt

I work in marketing

أنا أعمل فى التسويق

ana aA-mal fee al-tas-weeq

I'm retired

أنا متقاعد

ana mota-qaa-Aid

I'm self-employed

أنا أعمل لحسابى الخاص
ana aA-mal li-Hisaa-bee al-khaaS

I have two children

لدى طفلان
la-day-ya Tif-laan

we don't have any children

ليس لدينا أطفال
lay-sa la-day-na aT-faal

two boys and a girl

ولدان وبنت
waladaan wa bint

a boy of five and a girl of two

ولد عمره خمس سنوات وبنت عمرها سنتين
walad Aom-ro khams sanawaat wa bint Aom-raha sanatayn

have you ever been to Britain?

هل سبق لك السفر إلى بريطانيا ؟
hal sabaq laka al-safar ila bree-Tan-ya?/hal sabaq lakee al-safar ila bree-Tan-ya?

Understanding

هل أنت إنجليزى / إنجليزية؟
hal an-ta in-glee-zee/hal an-te in-glee-zay-ya?
are you English?

أنا أعرف إنجلترا جيداً
ana aA-rif inglatirra jay-yidan
I know England quite well

نحن أيضاً فى أجازة هنا
naH-noo ay-Dan fee ajaa-za hu-na
we're on holiday here too

أود زيارة اسكتلندا
awad-do ze-yaa-rat iskot-landa
I'd love to go to Scotland one day

TALKING ABOUT YOUR STAY

Expressing yourself

I'm here on business
أنا هنا فى مهمة عمل
ana hu-na fee mo-him-mat Aamal

we're on holiday
نحنُ فى أجازة
naH-noo fee ajaa-za

I arrived three days ago
وصلتُ منذ ثلاثة أيام
waSal-to mondh tha-laa-that ay-yaam

we've been here for a week
نحن هنا منذ أُسبوع
naH-noo hu-na mondh os-booA

I'm only here for a week
أنا هنا لمدة أُسبوع
ana hu-na le-mod-dat os-booA

we're just passing through
نحن نزور المكان فقط ولا نقيم هنا
naH-noo nazoor al-makaan faqaT wala no-qeem hu-na

this is our first time in Egypt
هذه أول مرة نزور فيها مصر
ha-dhe-he aw-wal mar-ra nazoor fee-ha miSr

we're here to celebrate our wedding anniversary
نحن هنا لنحتفل بعيد زواجنا
naH-noo hu-na le-naH-tafil bi-Aeed za-waaj-na

we're on our honeymoon
نحن فى شهر العسل
naH-noo fee shahr al-Aasal

we're here with friends
نحن هنا مع بعض الأصدقاء
naH-noo hu-na maAa baAD al-aS-deqaa'

we're touring around

نحن نقوم بجولة
naH-noo na-qoom bi-jow-la

we managed to get a cheap flight

حصلنا على رحلة طيران رخيصة
HaSal-na Ala riH-lat Taya-raan ra-khee-Sa

we're thinking about buying a house here

نحن نفكر في شراء منزل هنا
naH-noo no-fak-kir fee she-raa' man-zil hu-na

Understanding

استمتع بإقامتك!
is-tam-tiA bi-iqaa-matak/is-tam-tiAee bi-iqaa-matik
enjoy your stay!

إستمتع / إستمتعي بباقي أجازتك
is-tam-tiA/is-tam-tiAee be-baa-qee ajaz-tak
enjoy the rest of your holiday!

هل هذه أول زيارة لك إلى الاقصر؟
hal ha-dhe-he aw-wal ze-ya-ra lak ila al-oq-Sor?
is this your first time in Luxor?

كم ستمكث؟
kam sa-tam-koth?
how long are you staying?

هل تحب الإقامة هنا؟
hal to-Hib al-iqaa-ma hu-na?
do you like it here?

هل سبق لك / لك زيارة ..؟
hal sabaqa laka/lakee ze-yaa-rat...?
have you been to ...?

STAYING IN TOUCH

Expressing yourself

we should stay in touch

يجب أن نبقى على إتصال

ya-jib ann nab-qaa Ala it-tiSaal

I'll give you my e-mail address

سوف أعطيك عنوان بريدى الألكترونى

sow-fa oA-Tee-ka/oA-Tee-kee Aon-waan ba-ree-dee al-elek-troo-nee

here's my address, in case you ever come to Britain

هذا عنوانى اذا أتيت لزيارة بريطانيا

ha-dha Aon-waa-nee edha atay-ta/atay-tee li-ze-yaa-rat bree-Tan-ya

Understanding

مكن تعطينى عنوانك؟

mom-kin taA-Te-ne An-oo-a-nak?

will you give me your address?

هل عندك بريد ألكترونى؟

hal Aan-dak ba-reed elek-troo-nee?

do you have an e-mail address?

مرحبا بك فى أى وقت لتأتى وتقيم معنا هنا

mar-Haban bika fee ay waqt li-ta'-tee wa to-qeem maAa-na hu-na

you're always welcome to come and stay with us here

EXPRESSING YOUR OPINION

> **Some informal expressions**
>
> كان هذا مملاً *ka-na ha-dha mo-mill-lan* it was boring
>
> أنا تعبان *ana taA-baan* I feel tired

Expressing yourself

I really like ...
أنا فعلاً أُريدُ ...
ana fiA-lan o-reed ...

I really liked ...
أنا فعلاً أردتُ ...
ana fiA-lan arad-to ...

I don't like ...
أنا لا أحبُ ...
ana laa o-Hibb ...

I didn't like ...
أنا لم أحبُ ...
ana lam o-Hibb ...

I love ...
أنا أحب ...
ana o-Hibb ...

I loved ...
أنا أحببت ...
ana aH-bab-to ...

I would like ...
أنا أود ...
ana awad-do ...

I would have liked ...
كنت أمنى ...
kon-to ataman-na ...

I find it ...
إنّها ...
in-naha...

I found it ...
لقد كانت ...
laqad kaa-nat...

it's lovely
إنّها رائعة
in-naha raa-'iAa

it was lovely
لقد كانت رائعة
laqad kaa-nat raa-'iAa

I agree
أنا أوافق
ana o-waa-fiq

I don't agree
أنا لا أوافق
ana laa o-waa-fiq

I don't know
لا أدري
laa ad-ree

I don't mind
ليس لدي مانع
lay-sa laday-ya maa-niA

I don't like the sound of it
لا أحبّ هذا بتاتاً
laa o-Hibb ha-dha ba-taa-tan

it sounds interesting
يبدوا مثيراً
yab-doo ha-dha mothee-ran

it really annoys me
هذا يزعجني جدا
ha-dha yoz-Aej-nee jid-dan

it was boring
كان ذلك مملاً
kaa-na dha-lika momil-lan

it's a rip-off
هذه نصب
ha-dha naSb

it gets very busy at night
هذا المكان يكون مزدحماً في الليل
ha-dha al-makaan yakoon moz-daHim jid-dan fee al-layl

it's too busy
هذا المكان مزدحم جداً
ha-dha al-makaan moz-daHim jid-dan

it's very quiet

هذا المكان هادئ جداً

ha-dha al-makaan haa-di' jid-dan

I really enjoyed myself

لقد استمتعتُ حقاً

laqad is-tam-taA-to Haq-qan

we had a great time

قضينا وقتاً رائعاً

qaDay-na waq-tan raa-'iAan

there was a really good atmosphere

كان المكان جميلاً حقاً

kaa-na al-makaan ja-mee-lan Haq-qan

we met some nice people

قابلنا بعض الناس اللطفاء

qaa-bal-na baAD al-naas al-loTa-faa'

we found a great hotel

وجدنا فندقاً ممتازاً

wajad-na fon-doq mom-taaz

Understanding

هل تُحبُ ...؟

hal to-Hib...?/hal to-Hib-be ...?

do you like ...?

هل استمتعتَ بوقتك؟

hal is-tam-tAt bi-waq-tak?/hal is-tam-taA-te bi-waq-tik?

did you enjoy yourselves?

يجب أن تذهب إلى ....

ya-jib ann tadh-hab ila ...

you should go to ...

أنا أُرشِّح ...

ana o-rash-shiH ...

I recommend ...

إنها منطقة رائعة
in-naha man-Tiqa raa-'iAh
it's a lovely area

ليس هناك الكثيرُ من السيّاح
lay-sa hu-nak al-ka-theer min al-soy-yaaH
there aren't too many tourists

لاتذهب أثناء العطلة الأسبوعية لتجنب الازدحام الشديد
la-tadh-hab ath-na' al-AoT-la al-os-boo-Aay-ay li-ta-jan-nob al-izde-Haam al-sha-deed
don't go at the weekend, it's too busy

هذا السعر مُغالي فيه بعض الشّيء
ha-dha al-siAr mo-gha-la feeh baAD al-shay'
it's a bit overrated

TALKING ABOUT THE WEATHER

> ### Some informal expressions
> الجو حر *ej-jow Harr* it's scorching!
> الجو برد *ej-jow bard* it's freezing!
> الجو فيه شبورة *ej-jow feeh shab-boora* it's foggy
> انا حرّان / حرانه *ana Har-raan* I'm boiling
> أنا سقعان / سقعانه *ana Har-raa-na* I'm freezing

Expressing yourself

have you seen the weather forecast for tomorrow?
ما هي توقعات الارصاد لطقس الغد؟
maa he-ya tawaq-qoAaat al-ar-Saad li-Tas al-ghadd?

it's going to be nice
سيكون الطقسُ لطيف
sa-yakoon al-Taqs la-Teef

it isn't going to be nice
لن يكون الطقسُ لطيف
lan yakoon al-Taqs la-Teef

it's really hot
الطقس حار جداً
al-Taqs Haar jid-dan

it gets cold at night
يكون الطقسُ بارد في الليل
yakoon al-Taqs baa-rid fee al-layl

the weather was beautiful
كان الطقسُ رائع
kaa-na al-Taqs raa-'iA

it rained a few times
لقد أمطرت عدة مرات
laqad am-Tarat Aid-dat mar-raat

there was a thunderstorm
كان هناك عاصفة رعدية
kaa-na hu-nak Aaa-Sifa raA-day-ya

it's been lovely all week
كان الطقسُ جميل طيلة الأسبوع
kaa-na al-Taqs ja-meel Tee-lat al-os-booA

it's very humid here
إن الجوَ به رطوبة عالية هنا
in-na al-jow be-he ro-Too-ba Aaa-lay-ya hu-na

Understanding

من المتوقع أن تُمطر
min al-motawaq-qaA ann tom-Tir
it's supposed to rain

توقعات الأرصاد تشير بأن الطقسَ سيكون جيد بقية الأسبوع
ta-waq-qoAaat al-ar-Saad to-sheer an-na al-Taqs sa-ya-koon jay-yid ba-qay-yat al-os-booA
they've forecast good weather for the rest of the week

سيكون الطقسُ حار غداً
sa-ya-koon al-Taqs Haar ghadan
it will be hot again tomorrow

TRAVELLING

The basics

airport	مطار	*maTaar*
boarding	الصعود إلى الطّائرة	*al-So-Aood ila al-Taa-'e-ra*
boarding card	بطاقة صعود الطّائرة	*be-Taa-qat So-Aood al-Taa-'e-ra*
boat	مركب	*mar-kib*
bus	حافلة	*Hafila*
bus station	محطّة حافلة	*maHaT-Tat Hafila*
bus stop	موقف حافلة	*mow-qaf Hafila*
car	سيّارة	*say-ya-ra*
check-in	دخول	*do-khool*
coach	اوتوبيس	*oto-bees*
ferry	عبّارة	*Aab-baa-ra*
flight	رحلة	*riH-la*
gate	بوّابة	*bow-waa-ba*
left-luggage (office)	(مكتب) الحقائب المتروكة	*(mak-tab) al-Haqaa-'ib al-mat-roo-ka*
luggage	حقائب	*Haqaa-'ib*
map	خريطة	*kha-ree-Ta*
motorway	طريق سريع	*Ta-reeq sa-reeA*
passport	جواز سفر	*jawaaz safar*
plane	طائرة	*Taa-'e-ra*
platform	رصيف	*ra-Seef*
railway station	محطّة سكة حديد	*maHaT-Tat sik-ka Hadeed*
return (ticket)	تذكرة ذهاب وإياب	*tadh-kara dhe-haab wa ee-yaab*
road	طريق	*Ta-reeq*
shuttle bus	أتوبيس المطار	*oto-bees al-maTaar*
single (ticket)	ذهاب	*dhi-haab*
street	شارع	*shaa-riA*
street map	خريطة الشوارع	*kha-ree-Tat al-shawaa-riA*
taxi	تاكسى	*tak-see*
terminal	محطّة	*maHaT-Ta*
to book	يحجز	*yaH-jiz*
to check in	تسجيل الدخول	*tas-jeel al-do-khool*
to hire	يستأجر	*yas-ta'-jir*

Expressing yourself

where can I buy tickets?
أين مكتب شراء التّذاكر؟
ayna mak-tab she-raa' al-ta-dhaa-kir?

a ticket to ..., please
تذكرة إلى ... من فضلك
tadh-kara ila ... min faD-lak

I'd like to book a ticket
أريد حجز تذكرة
o-reed Hajz tadh-kara

how much is a ticket to ...?
كم ثمن تذكرة إلى ...؟
kam thaman tadh-kara ila ...?

are there any concessions for students?
هل يوجد تذاكر مخفضة للطلبة؟
hal yoo-jad ta-dhaa-kir mokhaf-faDa lil-Talaba?

could I have a timetable, please?
أريد جدول مواعيد السفر من فضلك؟
o-reed jad-wal mawa-Aeed al-safar min faD-lak?

is there an earlier/later one
هل يوجد موعد قبل / بعد هذا؟
hal yoo-jad maw-Aid qabl/baAd ha-dha?

how long does the journey take?
كم تستغرق الرحلة؟
kam tas-tagh-riq al-riH-la?

is this seat free?
هل هذا المقعد خالي؟
hal ha-dha al-maq-Aad khaa-lee?

I'm sorry, there's someone sitting there
أنا آسف. هذاالمقعد غير خال
ana aa-sif/aa-sifa ha-dha al-maq-Aad ghayr khaa-lee

Understanding

وصول	arrivals
ملغي	cancelled
رحلات غير مباشرة	connections
مغادرة	departures
دخول	entrance
ممنوع الدخول	no entry
استعلامات	information
متأخِّر	delayed
خروج	exit
حمّام	toilets
رجال	gents
سيِّدات	ladies
تذاكر	tickets

لا يوجد أماكن شاغرة
laa yoo-jad amaa-kin shaa-ghira
everything is fully booked

BY PLANE

Always check visa requirements with the embassy of the country you are visiting. Some countries such as Egypt will allow UK visitors to obtain a visa upon arrival at the airport, but others may require that you are in possession of a visa before travelling to ensure entry into the country.

Most major airlines operate flights out of London, all of which are more numerous over the summer tourist months, especially to resorts such as Sharm El-Sheikh, Luxor and Hurghada in Egypt.

Expressing yourself

where's the British Airways check-in?
أين فحص تذاكر السفرعلي الخطوط الجوّية البريطانية؟
ayna faHS tadhaa-kir al-safar Ala al-khoTooT al-jow-way-ya al-breeTa-nay-ya?

I've got an e-ticket
معي تذكرة الكترونية
maAee tadh-kara elek-tro-nay-ya

one suitcase and one piece of hand luggage
شنطة كبيرة وحقيبة يد
shan-Ta ka-bee-ra wa Haqee-bat yadd

what time do we board?
متى نصعد الطّائرة؟
mata naS-Aad al-Taa-'e-ra?

I'd like to confirm my return flight
أريد تأكيد موعد رحلة العودة
o-reed ta'-keed mow-Aed riH-lat al-Aow-da

one of my suitcases is missing
فقدت حقيبة كبيرة
faqad-to Haqee-ba kabee-ra

my luggage hasn't arrived
لم تصل حقائبي بعد
lam ta-Sil Haqaa-ebee baAd

the plane was two hours late
تأخرت الطّائرة ساعتين
ta-'akh-kharat al-Taa-'e-ra saa-Aatayn

I've missed my connection
فاتني موعد رحلة الربط
faa-tanee mow-Aed riH-lat al-rabT

I've left something on the plane
تركت شيئا بالطّائرة
tarak-to shay-'an bel-Taa-'e-ra

I want to report the loss of my luggage

أريد الإبلاغ عن فقد حقائبي
o-reed al-ib-laagh An faqd Haqaa-ebee

Understanding

إسترداد الحقائب	baggage reclaim
تسجيل الدخول	check-in
جمارك	Customs
صالة المغادرة	departure lounge
رحلات داخلية	domestic flights
معفى من الجمارك	duty free
بضائع عليها جمارك	goods to declare
صعود فوري للطائرة	immediate boarding
بضائع ليس عليها جمارك	nothing to declare
فحص الجوازات	passport control

من فضلك انتظر فى صالة المغادرة
min faD-lak in-taZir fee Saa-lat al-mogha-dara
please wait in the departure lounge

هل تريد مقعد بجانب النافذة أو على الممر؟
hal to-reed maq-Aad bija-nib al-na-fidha aw Ala al-mamarr?
would you like a window seat or an aisle seat?

يجب عليك أن تغيِّر الرحلة فى ...
ya-jib Aalay-ka an to-ghay-yir al-riH-la fee …
you'll have to change in …

كم حقيبة معك؟
kam Haqee-ba maAak?
how many bags do you have?

هل حزمت حقائبك بنفسك؟
hal Hazam-ta/Hazam-te Haqaa-ebak bi-naf-sak?
did you pack all your bags yourself?

هل أعطاك أحد شيئاً لتأخذه معك على الطائرة؟
hal aA-Taa-ka /aA-taa-ke aHad shay' li-ta'-kho-dho /li-ta'-kho-dheeh ma-Aak Ala al-Taa-'e-ra?
has anyone given you anything to take on board?

حقيبتك بها خمسة كيلو وزن زائد
Haqee-batak bi-ha khamsa kee-loo wazn zaa-'id
your luggage is five kilos overweight

هذا هو كارت صعود الطائرة
ha-dha hu-wa kart So-Aood al-Taa-'e-ra
here's your boarding card

يبدأ صعود الطائرة الساعة ...
yab-da' So-Aood al-Taa-'e-ra al-saa-Aa ...
boarding will begin at ...

من فضلك تقدم نحو بوابة رقم ...
min faD-lak taqad-dam naH-wa bow-waa-ba raqam ...
please proceed to gate number ...

هذا هو أخر نداء للركاب المغادرين الي ...
ha-dha hu-wa aa-khir ni-daa' lil-rok-kaab al-moghaa-direen ila ...
this is a final call for ...

يمكن أن تتصل بهذا الرقم للتأكد من وصول حقائبك
yom-kin an tat-taSil bi-ha-dha al-raqam lil-ta'k-kod min wo-Sool Haqaa-'e-bak
you can call this number to check if your luggage has arrived

BY BUS, TAXI, TRAIN

Buses are very safe and clean, although not the fastest mode of transport.
Tickets can be purchased on the bus when you begin your journey; you
can, however, often buy books of tickets in advance.

Another popular means of transport for shorter journeys is the micro-bus,
a type of minibus that picks people up at the side of the road and follows
set routes; you simply ask to get off when you reach your destination. Be
sure to check that the driver is going in the direction you want to go! Once
you have found a seat on the micro-bus you can pass your payment up to
the driver.

Taxis are also very common; you can call for one to come and pick you up, but this works out significantly more expensive than hailing one in the street. You can hail a taxi anywhere on the street; they will always have a "taxi" sign on top and usually a different coloured licence plate from other cars. If the taxi does not have a meter then you should agree a price with the driver before setting off.

If you are travelling a long distance within the country, or even travelling to another country, one of the fastest and cheapest ways to travel is by car. Typically found near bus stations, many taxis travel to specific destinations, for example from Cairo to Alexandria. The driver will usually wait until the car is full before leaving. If you do not feel comfortable being stuck in a car with four or five other people then you can pay the driver extra to have the seat beside you kept free. If you are with a small group you can negotiate a price.

Travelling by rail in Egypt is cheap, safe and easy and there can be wonderful views to enjoy from the comfort of your carriage, particularly on routes from Cairo to Alexandria or Aswan.

Expressing yourself

what time is the next train to ...?
ما هو موعد القطار القادم ...؟
maa hu-wa mow-Aed al-qe-Taar al-qaa-dim ...?

what time is the last train?
ما هو موعد اخر قطار؟
maa hu-wa mow-Aed aa-khir qe-Taar?

which platform is it for ...?
أين الرصيف المتجه إلي ...؟
ayna al-ra-Seef al-mot-ta-jih ila ...?

where can I catch a bus to ...?
أين آخذ الحافلة المتجهة إلى ...؟
ayna aa-khodh alHafila al-mot-ta-jiha ila ...?

is this the stop for ...?
هل هذه محطة الانتظار للذهاب الي ...؟
hal ha-dhe-he maHaT-Tat al-in-tiZaar lil-dhe-haab ila ...?

is this where the coach leaves for …?

هل هذا موقف إنتظار الحافلات المتجهة إلى …؟

hal ha-dha mow-qaf in-tiZaar al-oto-bees al-mot-tajih ila…?

can you tell me when I need to get off?

هل ممكن أن تخبرني متى أنزل؟

hal mom-kin an tokh-bir-nee ma-taa an-zil?

I've missed my train/bus

فاتني القطار / الحافلة

faa-tanee al-qi-Taar/al-Hafila

Understanding

إلى القطارات	to the trains
مكتب التَّذاكر	ticket office
تذاكر لسفر اليوم	tickets for travel today
أسبوعي	weekly
شهري	monthly
حجز اليوم	for the day
حجوزات	bookings

هناك محطَّة تبعد قليلا باتجاه اليمين

hu-naak maHaT-Ta tab-Aod qalee-lan bit-tijah al-yameen

there's a stop a bit further along on the right

يجب عليك أن تغيرالرحلة في محطة …

ya-jib Aalay-ka ann to-ghay-yir al-riH-la fee maHaT-Tat …

you'll have to change at …

تحتاج أن تستقل حافلة رقم …

taH-taaj ann tasta-qill Hafila raqam …

you need to get the number … bus

هذا القطار يتوقف في …

ha-dha al-qi-Taar yatawaq-qaf fee …

this train calls at …

بعد محطتين من هنا

baAd maHaT-Ta-tayn min hu-na

two stops from here

TRAVELLING

BY CAR

You can find most major international car hire companies throughout the Arabic-speaking world. It is important to remember that all Arab countries drive on the right-hand side of the road.

The road network in Egypt is adequate for travel, and few, if any, motorways have tolls. Motorists tend to be very helpful so if you get lost don't be shy to ask for help and directions.

Speed limits are posted on the major roads and highways in Egypt and are rigidly enforced.

Expressing yourself

where can I find a service station?
أين أجد إستراحة لخدمة المسافرين؟
ayna ajid is-tiraa-Ha li-khid-mat al-mo-saa-fireen

lead-free petrol, please
بنزين خالي من الرصاص من فضلك
ban-zeen khaa-lee min al-ro-SaaS min faD-lak

how much is it per litre?
كم ثمن اللتر؟
kam thaman al-litr?

we got stuck in a traffic jam
تعطلنا بسبب إزدحام المرور
taAaT-Tal-na bi-sabab iz-diHaam al-mo-roor

is there a garage near here?
هل يوجد ميكانيكي لإصلاح السيّارات بالقرب من هنا؟
hal yoo-jad mikaneeki le-iS-laaH al-say-ya-raat bel-qorb min hu-na?

can you help us to push the car?
ممكن تساعدنا لندفع السيّارة؟
mom-kin ti-saa-Aidna li-nad-faA al-say-ya-ra?

the battery's dead

البطارية فارغة تماما
al-baT-Taa-ray-ya faa-righa ta-maa-man

I've broken down

تعطلت سيّارتي
taAaT-Talat say-ya-ra-tee

we've run out of petrol

نفذ الوقود
nafidha al-wa-qood

I've got a puncture and my spare tyre is flat

أحد الإطارات به ثقب والإحتياطي فارغ
aHad al-eTaa-raat be-he thoqb wal al-iHte-yaa-Tee faa-righ

we've just had an accident

تعرضنا لحادث
taAar-raD-na li-Haa-dith

I've lost my car keys

فقدتُ مفاتيح سيّارتي
faqad-to mafaa-teeH say-ya-ra-tee

how long will it take to repair?

كم يستغرق إصلاحها؟
kam yas-tagh-riq iSlaa-Huha?

◆ Hiring a car

I'd like to hire a car for a week

أريد استئجار سيّارة لمدة أسبوع
o-reed is-ti'-jaar say-ya-ra le-mod-dat os-booA

an automatic (car)

سيّارة أوتوماتك
say-ya-ra auto-matik

do I have to fill the tank up before I return it?

هل يجب عليّ ملء الخزّان بالبنزين عند إعادة السيّارة؟
hal ya-jib Aalay-ya mal' al-khaz-zaan bil-ban-zeen Ain-da e-Aaa-dat al-say-ya-ra?

I'd like to take out comprehensive insurance

أريد تأمين شامل

o-reed ta'-meen shaa-mil

◆ Getting a taxi

is there a taxi rank near here?

هل يوجد موقف تاكسي بالقرب من هنا؟

hal yoo-jad mow-qaf tak-see bel qorb min hu-na?

I'd like to go to …

أريد الذهاب إلى...

o-reed al-dhe-haab ila …

I'd like to book a taxi for 8pm

أريد حجز تاكسي للساعة الثامنة مساءاً

o-reed Hajz tak-see lil-saa-Aa al-thaa-mina masaa-an

you can drop me off here, thanks

ممكن أنزل هنا. شكراً

mom-kin an-zil hu-na, shok-ran

how much will it be to go to the airport?

كم أجرة الذّهاب إلى المطار؟

kam oj-rat al-dhe-haab ila al-maTaar?

◆ Hitchhiking

I'm going to …

أريد الذهاب الي ...

o-reed al-dhe-haab ila…

can you drop me off here?

ممكن أنزل هنا؟

mom-kin an-zil hu-na?

could you take me as far as …?

ممكن توصلني الي ...؟

mom-kin to-waS-Sal-nee ila …?

thanks for the lift

شكراً علي التوصيلة

shok-ran Ala al-tow-See-la

TRAVELLING

we hitched a lift

حصلنا على توصيلة مجانية
HaSal-na Aala tow-See-la maj-jaa-nay-ya

Understanding

اتِّجاهات أخرى	other directions
لا يوجد أماكن	full (car park)
يوجد أماكن	spaces (car park)
احتفظ بالتذكرة	keep your ticket
تأجير سيّارات	car hire
مكان انتظار السيّارات	car park
خفّض السّرعة	slow
ممنوع انتظارالسيّارات	no parking
كل الإتِّجاهات	all directions
انتظار السيّارات بالأجر مكان	pay and display
التزم بالحارة	get in lane

أريد الإطّلاع على رخصة القيادة . ، إثبات الشخصيّة ، مايثبت العنوان وبطاقة الإئتمان
oo-reed al-iT-Ti-laaA Aala rokh-Sat al-qe-yaa-da, ith-baat al-shakh-Say-ya, ma-yoth-bit al-Aon-waan wa-bi-Taa-qat al-'i-te-man
I'll need your driving licence, another form of ID, proof of address and your credit card

يجب دفع مائة وخمسون جنيه قيمة التأمين
ya-jib dafA me-'a wa kham-soon je-neeh qee-mat al-ta'-meen
there's a 150-jeneeh deposit

حسنا. تفضل بالدخول. سأوصلك الي ...
Hasa-nan! tafaD-Dal bil-do-khool, sa-o-waS-Silak ila ...
all right, get in, I'll take you as far as ...

BY BOAT

Nile cruises, either on a cruise ship where lodging, food and entertainment are all provided, or on a felucca – a traditional sailing boat – are a very popular way of seeing Egypt. There are also numerous day trips available, offering activities such as fishing in the Red Sea or visiting islands off the Egyptian coast.

Expressing yourself

how long is the crossing?
كم يستغرق زمن العبور؟
kam yas-tagh-riq zaman al-Ao-boor?

I feel seasick
أشعر بدوار البحر
ash-Aor be-do-waar al-baHr

Understanding

للمسافرين بدون سيَّارات فقط	foot passengers only
موعد العبور التالى هو ...	next crossing at ...

ACCOMMODATION

Hotels throughout the Arab world vary in size, service and pricing. Given the importance of the tourist industry in countries such as Egypt and the United Arab Emirates, you will find it relatively easy to find accommodation to suit your budget. Egyptian hotels are rated with a star system from 1 to 5 but a 2- or 3-star establishment is likely to be comparable to a 1-star in the UK.

You will be able to book many package holidays or hotels online or through a travel agent in advance. Alternatively, airports have a number of reservation offices that will allow you to choose from a wide range of accommodation options. In all major cities you will also be able to find a local tourist office that can direct you to your desired accommodation.

If you're feeling adventurous, you can always try and find areas of the city with high concentrations of hotels. The advantage of these areas is that they are usually right in the heart of the city and offer decent rates. Most prices should be posted at the front desk. Always be sure to see your room beforehand to ensure that it meets your expectations.

Self-catering accommodation is another option and can offer excelent value for money, particularly if you're planning to spend a couple of weeks in the same city: the cost of renting a room for a month is sometimes the equivalent of staying three or four nights in a hotel!

To use any British appliances you will need the appropriate adaptor, which can be purchased either in the UK or in the country you are visiting. Electricity in Egypt uses 220 volts.

The basics

all-inclusive	شامل التكاليف	shaa-mil al-taka-leef
bath	بانيو	ban-yoo
bathroom	حمام	Ham-maam
bathroom with shower	حمام مع دش	Ham-maam maAa dosh
bed	سرير	sa-reer

bed and breakfast	مبيت وافطار *ma-beet wa if-Taar*
double bed	سرير مزدوج *sa-reer moz-dawaj*
double room	غرفة مزدوجة *ghor-fa moz-dawaja*
en-suite bathroom	غرفة حمام خاصة *ghor-fat Ham-maam khaaS-Sa*
family room	غرفة عائلية *ghor-fa Aaa-'e-lay-ya*
flat	شقة *shaq-qa*
full-board	اقامة كاملة *iqaa-ma kaa-mila*
half-board	نصف اقامة *neSf iqaa-ma*
hotel	فندق *fon-doq*
key	مفتاح *mof-taH*
rent	ايجار *ee-jaar*
self-catering	اقامة بدون وجبات *iqaa-ma be-doon waj-baat*
shower	دش *dosh*
single bed	سرير فردي *sa-reer far-dee*
single room	غرفة لشخص *ghor-fa li-shakhS*
tenant	مستأجر *mos-ta'-jir*
tent	خيمة *khay-ma*
toilets	حمام *Ham-maam*
youth hostel	بيت الشباب *bayt al-sha-baab*
to book	يحجز مسبقا *yaH-jiz mos-baqan*
to rent	يستأجر *yas-ta'-jir*
to reserve	يحجز *yaH-jiz*

Expressing yourself

I have a reservation

لدي حجز
laday-ya Hajz

the name's ...

الاسم هو ...
al-ism hu-wa ...

do you take credit cards?

هل يمكن الدفع ببطاقة الائتمان؟
hal yom-kin al-dafA be-beTaa-qat al-e'-ti-maan?

Understanding

اماكن شاغرة	vacancies
كامل العدد	full
خاص	private
استقبال	reception
حمام	toilets

لو سمحت..اريد الاطلاع على جواز سفرك!
low sa-maHt o-reed al-iT-TilaaA Aala jawaaz safarak!
could I see your passport, please?

قم بملء هذه الاستمارة!
qom bi-mal' ha-dhe-he al-is-timaara!
could you fill in this form?

HOTELS

Expressing yourself

do you have any vacancies?
هل يوجد اماكن شاغرة؟
hal yoo-jad amaa-kin shaa-ghira?

how much is a double room per night?
كم تكلفة الاقامة في غرفة مزدوجة في الليلة؟
kam tak-lifat al-iqaa-ma fee ghor-fa moz-dawaja fee al-lay-la?

I'd like to reserve a double room/a single room
اريد حجز غرفة مزدوجة / غرفة لشخص واحد
o-reed Hajz ghor-fa muz-dawaja/ghor-fa le-shakhS waa-Hid

for three nights
لثلاث ليالي
li-tha-laath la-yaa-lee

would it be possible to stay an extra night?
هل يمكن الاقامة لليلة اضافية؟
hal yom-kin al-iqaa-ma le-lay-la eDaa-fay-ya

ACCOMMODATION

46

do you have any rooms available for tonight?

هل يوجد غرف شاغرة هذه الليلة؟

hal yoo-jad ghor-fa shaa-ghira ha-dhe-he al-lay-la?

do you have any family rooms?

هل لديكم غرف عائلية؟

hal laday-kom gho-raf Aaa-'e-lay-ya?

would it be possible to add an extra bed?

هل يمكن وضع سرير اضافي؟

hal yom-kin waDA sa-reer eDaa-fee?

could I see the room first?

هل يمكن رؤية الغرفة اولا؟

hal yom-kin ro'-yat al-ghor-fa aw-walan?

do you have anything bigger/quieter?

هل يوجد مكان اوسع / اكثر هدوء؟

hal yoo-jad makaan aw-saA/ak-thar ho-doo'?

that's fine, I'll take it

.حسنا! ساخذ هذه

Hasa-nan! sa-aa-khoz ha-dhe-he

could you recommend any other hotels?

هل تعرف فندق اخرجيد؟

hal taA-rif fon-doq aa-khar jay-yid?

is breakfast included?

هل الاقامة شاملة الافطار؟

hal al-iqaa-ma shaa-mila al-if-Taar?

what time do you serve breakfast?

ما موعد تقديم الافطار؟

ma mow-Aed taq-deem al-if-Taar?

is there a lift?

هل يوجد مصعد؟

hal yoo-jad miS-Aad?

is the hotel near the centre of town?

هل الفندق قريب من وسط المدينة؟

hal al-fon-doq qa-reeb min wasaT al-madina?

what time will the room be ready?

متى تكون الغرفة جاهزة؟

mata takoon al-ghor-fa jaa-he-za?

the key for room ..., please

اريد مفتاح الغرفة من فضلك!

o-reed mof-taH al-ghor-fa min faD-lak!

could I have an extra blanket?

ممكن آخذ بطانية اضافية؟

mom-kin aa-khodh baT-Ta-nay-ya eDaa-fay-ya?

the air conditioning isn't working

مكيف الهواء لا يعمل.

mo-kay-yif al-hawa' la yaA-mal

Understanding

معذرة! كل الاماكن لدينا كاملة العدد.

maA-dhira! kol al-amaakin la-day-na kaa-milat al-Adad

I'm sorry, but we're full

لا يوجد لدينا الان سوى غرفة لشخص واحد.

la yoo-jad laday-na al-aan so-wa ghor-fa li-shakhS waa-Hid

we only have a single room available

كم ليلة؟

kam lay-la?

how many nights is it for?

لو سمحت! ما هو اسمك؟

low sa-maHt! ma hu-wa is-mak?/low sa-matl-te! ma hu-wa is-mik?

what's your name, please?

التسجيل واستلام الغرف من منتصف النهار.

al-tas-jeel wa is-ti-laam al-gho-raf min mon-taSaf al-na-haar

check-in is from midday

يجب سداد الفاتورة والمغادرة قبل الساعة الحادية عشر

ya-jib sa-daad al-fa-too-ra wa al-mogha-dara qabl al-saa-Aa al-Ha-de-ya Ashar

you have to check out before 11 am

الافطار بالمطعم ما بين الساعة السابعة والنصف والساعة التاسعة.
al-if-Taar bil-maT-Am ma bayn al-saa-Aa al-sa-bi-Ah wa-neSf wa al-saa-Aa al-taa-seAa
breakfast is served in the restaurant between 7.30 and 9.00

هل تريد جرائد بالغرفة؟
hal to-reed jaraa-ed bil-ghor-fa?
would you like a newspaper in the morning?

لو سمحت! غرفتك ليست جاهزة
low sa-maHt! ghor-fatak lay-sat jaa-hiza
your room isn't ready yet

هل استخدمت البار الذي بالغرفة؟
hal is-takh-damt al-bar al-la-dhee bil ghor-fa?
have you used the minibar?

يمكن ترك اغراضك هنا.
yom-kin tar agh-raa-Dak hu-na
you can leave your bags here

YOUTH HOSTELS

Expressing yourself

do you have space for two people for tonight?
هل يوجد مكان لشخصين هذه الليلة؟
hal yoo-jad makaan li-shakh-Sayn ha-dhe-he al-lay-la?

we've booked two beds for three nights
لدينا حجز سريرين لمدة ثلاث ليالي هنا
laday-na Hajz sa-ree-rayn li-mod-dat tha-laath la-yaal-lee hu-na

could I leave my backpack at reception?
هل يمكن ترك حقيبة الظهر بالاستقبال؟
hal yom-kin tark Haqee-bat al-Zahr bel-is-tiq-baal?

do you have somewhere we could leave our bikes?
هل يوجد مكان لترك الدراجات؟
hal yoo-jad makaan li-tark al-dar-ra-jaat?

I'll come back for it around 7 o'clock

.سوف اعود لاستلامها حوالي الساعة السابعة

sow-fa a-Aood li-is-tilaa-me-ha Ha-waa-lee al-saa-Aa al-sa-bi-Aa

there's no hot water

.لا يوجد ماء ساخن

la yoo-jad maa' saa-kin

the sink's blocked

.حوض الغسيل مسدود

howD al-gha-seel mas-dood

Understanding

هل لديك بطاقة عضوية؟

hal laday-ka be-Taa-qat Aod-way-ya?

do you have a membership card?

السرير مزود بالمفارش

al-sa-reer mo-zow-wad bel-ma-faa-rish

bed linen is provided

المبيت مفتوح الساعة السادسة مساءا

al-ma-beet maf-tooH al-saa-Aa al-saa-disa ma-saa-'an

the hostel reopens at 6pm

SELF-CATERING

Expressing yourself

we're looking for somewhere to rent near a town

نريد استئجار مكان قريب من المدينة

no-reed is-ti'-jaar makaan qa-reeb min al-ma-dee-na

where do we pick up/leave the keys?

اين يمكن استلام / تسليم المفاتيح؟

ayna yom-kin is-tilaam/tas-leem al-mafaa-teeH?

is electricity included in the price?

هل السعر شامل فاتورة الكهرباء؟

hal al-siAr shaa-mil fa-too-rat al-kah-ra-ba'?

are bed linen and towels provided?

هل اماكن الاقامة بها مفارش سرير و فوط؟

hal amaakin al-iqaa-ma be-ha mafia-rish sa-reer wa fo-waT?

is a car necessary?

هل ضروري وجود سيارة؟

hal Da-roo-ree wo-jood say-ya-ra?

is there a pool?

هل يوجد حمام سباحة؟

hal yoo-jad Ham-maam se-baa-Ha?

is the accommodation suitable for elderly people?

هل مكان السكن مناسب لكبار السن؟

hal makaan al-sakan mo-naa-sib li-ke-baar al-sinn?

where is the nearest supermarket?

اين اقرب مكان للتسوق؟

ayna aq-rab makaan lil-tasow-woq?

Understanding

رجاء ترك المنزل نظيف ومرتب عند المغادرة!

ra-jaa' tark al-man-zil naZeef wa mo-rat-tab Aen-da al-mogha-dara

please leave the house clean and tidy after you leave

المنزل كامل التجهيز

al-man-zil kaa-mil al-taj-heez

the house is fully furnished

السعر شامل كل التكاليف.

al-siAr shaa-mil koll al-taka-leef

everything is included in the price

يلزم وجود سيارة للسكن في هذه المنطقة.

yal-zam wo-jood say-ya-ra lil-sakan fee ha-dhe-he al-man-Ti-qa

you really need a car in this part of the country

You will have no problem satisfying your appetite while travelling through the Arab world. Whether at a fancy restaurant in glitzy Dubai or a vendor in Cairo's bustling markets, you will be able to discover the richness of Arab cuisine in its many forms. You will find that eating out in a restaurant takes much more time than in the UK. This is not because of poor service, but rather because people in Arab countries tend to take their time over their food, enjoying lively and unhurried conversation as they eat.

Unless you are eating at a foreign restaurant, you will not typically find a set menu as meals do not follow the familiar pattern of starter, main course then dessert. Instead, you typically order a number of appetizers to be shared with everyone at the table. After the appetizers a main course will be offered, then dessert or fruit, then coffee or tea. It is not uncommon to share your food with others at your table.

At the end of your meal (or even during!) some places will offer you playing cards or backgammon tables to entertain yourselves. Unlike restaurants in the UK, there is no pressure to leave once you have finished eating, assuming you are sipping on something hot and enjoying your night.

If you feel like something a little less formal, then you can always buy a sandwich or snack from a street vendor or small restaurant. The Arab diet is not based on large-portioned meals so you will easily find snacks that are both filling and convenient to eat.

Many people in the Arab world tend to eat supper late in the evening. It is not uncommon for an evening out to begin at 9pm and end after midnight. Most restaurants will open for lunch until around 3 or 4pm, and will then close to prepare for the evening customers who start to come in around 7pm.

If you want a change from the local food, you can find fast-food restaurants almost anywhere. If you just want a cup of tea or coffee and a chat, there are a number of coffee houses in most towns, many of which serve shisha (flavoured tobacco pipes) to customers. Although most menus will have items priced, if you see a menu without a price don't be afraid to ask the waiter. If you have any special dietary requirements be sure to talk to the waiter about them. Tipping is encouraged and usually expected.

Although alcohol is not usually consumed in traditional restaurants, it is not difficult to find restaurants which do serve alcoholic drinks, particularly in more upmarket areas, star-rated hotels and tourist resorts.

The basics

beer	بيره	bee-ra
bill	فاتورة الحساب	fa-too-rat al-Hi-sab
black coffee	قهوة بدون حليب	qah-wa be-doon Ha-leeb
bottle	زجاجة	zojaa-ja
bread	خبز	khobz
breakfast	إفطار	if-Taar
coffee	قهوة	qah-wa
Coke®	كوكا	koke
dessert	طبق الحلو	Tabaq al-Helo
dinner	العشاء	al-Aashaa'
fruit juice	عصير فواكه	Aa-seer fawa-kih
lunch	الغذاء	al-ghadha'
menu	قائمة الطعام	qa-'imat al-Ta-Aaam
mineral water	مياه معدنية	mee-yah maA-danay-ya
red wine	خمر أحمر	khamr aH-mar
salad	سلطة	salaTa
sandwich	ساندويتش	sandwich
service	خدمة	khid-ma
sparkling (water, wine)	غازي	gha-zee
starter	مقبلات	mo-qab-be-laat
still (water)	غير فوار	ghayr fow-waar
tea	شاي	shaay
tip	بقشيش	baq-sheesh
water	ماء	maa'
white coffee	قهوة بالحليب	qah-wa bil-Ha-leeb
white wine	خمر أبيض	khamr ab-yaD
wine	خمر	khamr

EATING AND DRINKING

53

wine list	qaa-'i-mat al-kho-moor قائمة الخمور
to eat	ya'-kol يأكل
to have breakfast	yatana-wal al-if-Taar يتناول الإفطار
to have dinner	yatana-wal al-Aashaa' يتناول العشاء
to have lunch	yatana-wal al-ghada' يتناول الغداء
to order	yaT-lob يطلب

Expressing yourself

shall we go and have something to eat?

هل تريد الخروج لنأكل؟
hal to-reed al-kho-rooj li-na'-kol?

do you want to go for a drink?

هل تريد الخروج لنشرب شيئا؟
hal to-reed al-kho-rooj li-nash-rab shay-'an?

can you recommend a good restaurant?

هل تعرف مطعم جيد؟
hal taA-rif maT-Aam jay-yid?

I'm not very hungry

لست جائعا جداً
lasto jaa-'iAan jid-dan

excuse me!

لو سمحت!
low sa-maH-te!

cheers!

فى صحتك!
fee SiH-He-tik!

that was lovely

كان ذلك رائعا!
kaa-na dha-leka ra-'iAan!

could you bring us an ashtray, please?

نريد طفاية سجائر!
no-reed Taf-fa-yat sa-jaa-'ir, min faD-lak

where are the toilets, please?

أين الحمام من فضلك؟
ayna al-Ham-maam min faD-lak?

Understanding

تيك اواي   takeaway

RESERVING A TABLE

Expressing yourself

I'd like to reserve a table for tomorrow evening

أريد حجز طاولة لمساء الغد

o-reed Hajz Taa-wela li-ma-saa' al-ghad

for two people

لشخصين

li-shakh-Sayn

around 8 o'clock

حوالي الساعة الثامنة

Ha-waa-lee al-saa-Aa al-thaa-mina

do you have a table available any earlier than that?

هل يوجد طاولة قبل هذاالوقت؟

hal yoo-jad Taa-wela qabl ha-dha al-waqt?

I've reserved a table – the name's …

...حجزت طاولة و الأسم هو

Hajaz-to Taa-wela wa al-ism hu-wa …

Understanding

محجوز   reserved

في اي وقت؟

fee ayy waqt?

for what time?

كم فرد؟

kam fard?

for how many people?

55

ماالإسم؟
maa al-ism?
what's the name?

مدخنين أم غير مدخنين؟
modakh-khe-neen am ghayr modakh-khe-neen?
smoking or non-smoking?

هل لديك حجز؟
hal laday-ka Hajz?
do you have a reservation?

هل هذه الطاولة التي بالزاوية تناسبك؟
hal ha-dhe-he al-Taa-wela al-la-tee bel-zaa-we-ya to-na si-bok?
is this table in the corner OK for you?

معذرة، ليس لدينا أماكن متاحة الآن!
maA-dhira. lay-sa laday-na amaakin motaa-Ha al-aan!
I'm afraid we're full at the moment

ORDERING FOOD

Expressing yourself

yes, we're ready to order

نعم نحن جاهزون لطلب الطعام
naAm. naH-no jaa-hizoon li-Talab al-Ta-Aam

no, could you give us a few more minutes?

لا.نريد بعض الوقت لنختار؟
laa. no-reed baAD al-waqt li-nakh-taar?

I'd like ...

أريد ...
o-reed ...

could I have ...?

مكن أطلب ...
mom-kin aT-lob ...?

I'm not sure, what's "falafil"?

لست أعرف ما هي الفلافل
lasto aA-rif maa he-ya al-fa-laa-fil

I'll have that

سوف أتناول هذا
sow-fa atanaa-wal ha-dha

does it come with vegetables?

هل يقدم معه خضروات؟
hal yo-qad-dam maAa-ho khoDra-waat?

what desserts do you have?

ماهي اطباق الحلو لديكم؟
maa he-ya aT-baaq al-Hilo laday-kom?

some water, please

نريد ماء لوسمحت!
no-reed maa', lowsa-maHt!

a bottle of red/white wine

زجاجة خمر أحمر / أبيض
zojaa-jat khamr aH-mar/ab-yaD

that's for me

هذا لي
ha-dha lee

this isn't what I ordered, I wanted …

هذا ليس ماطلبته أنا أريد ...
ha-dha lay-sa ma Talab-toh. ana o-reed...

could we have some more bread, please?

لو سمحت. ممكن خبز زيادة؟
low sa-maHt! mom-kin khobz ze-yaa-da?

could you bring us another jug of water, please?

ممكن كوب ماء كبير من فضلك؟
mom-kin koob maa' ka-beer, min faD-lak?

Understanding

هل تريد طلب الطعام الآن؟
hal to-reed Talab al-Ta-Aam al-aan?
are you ready to order?

سأعود بعد قليل
sa-aAood baAd qa-leel
I'll come back in a few minutes

اسف. ليس لدينا مزيد من ...
aa-sef. lay-sa laday-na ma-zeed min ...
I'm sorry, we don't have any ... left

ماذا تريد أن تشرب؟
ma-dha to-reed an tash-rab?
what would you like to drink?

هل تريد طبق حلو أو قهوة؟
hal to-reed Tabaq Hilo aw qah-wa?
would you like dessert or coffee?

هل كان كل شيئ تمام؟
hal kaan kol shay' ta-maam
was everything OK?

BARS AND CAFÉS

Expressing yourself

I'd like ...
أريد ...
o-reed ...

a Coke®/a diet Coke®
كوكاكولا دايت
coca/coca diet

a glass of white/red wine
كأس خمرأبيض / أحمر
ka's khamr ab-yaD/aH-mar

a black/white coffee

قهوة بحليب/قهوة بدون حليب
qah-wa be-Ha-leeb/qah-wa be-doon Ha-leeb

a cup of tea

كوب شاي
koob shaay

the same again, please

نفس الطلب تاني لو سمحت
nafs al-Talab taa-nee, low sa-maHt

Understanding

خالي من الكحول   non-alcoholic

تحب تاخد إيه؟
te-Hibb ta-khod eeh?
what would you like?

مكن تدفع الآن. من فضلك؟
mom-kin tid-fA al-aan, min faD-lak?
could I ask you to pay now, please?

THE BILL

Expressing yourself

the bill, please

أريد الفاتورة من فضلك!
o-reed al-fa-too-ra min faD-lak!

how much do I owe you?

كم يجب أن أدفع لك؟
kam ya-jib an ad-fA lak?

do you take credit cards?

هل تقبل الدفع ببطاقة الائتمان؟
hal taq-bal al-dafA be-bi-Ta-qat al-'e-ti-maan?

I think there's a mistake in the bill

هناك خطأ فى الفاتورة

hunaa-ka khaT' fi al-fa-too-ra

is service included?

هل السعر شامل الخدمة؟

hal al-siAr shaa-mil al-khid-ma?

Understanding

هل ستدفعون الحساب معا؟

hal sa-tadfa-Aoon al-Hi-saab maAan?

are you all paying together?

نعم السعر يشمل الخدمة

naAam. al-siAr shaa-mil al-khid-ma

yes, service is included

FOOD AND DRINK

Understanding

نصف سوي	medium rare
مطهو جيّداً	well done
مسلوق	boiled
مقطّع مكعبات	chopped
مقطّع شرائح	sliced
سايح	melted
محمّر	fried
مدخّن	smoked
مشوي	grilled
مكسو بالسميط	breaded
نيء	rare
مملّح	salted
مجفّف	dried
مبخّر	steamed

◆ breakfast

زبدة	butter
خبز (عيش)	bread
توست	toast
قهوة	coffee
مربى	jam
عصير	juice
عسل	honey
زبادي	yogurt
فول مدمّس	fava beans
بيض	eggs
جبنة	cheese
زيتون	olives
زيت زيتون	olive oil
خضروات	vegetables

◆ snacks

Snacks can be bought in restaurants or from street vendors and often come served in a small wrap of paper so that you can eat on the run. You will usually find these snacks for sale at what is called a *forn* (literally, an oven).

سمبوسك بالجبنة	cheese turnovers
سمبوسك باللحمة	meat turnovers
فطيرة بالخضروات	vegetable pies
فطيرة سبانخ	spinach pies
فطيرة بالجبنة	cheese pies
سندوتش فول	falafel sandwich

◆ appetizers, salads and soups

These dishes can all be eaten as accompaniments to larger meals or as a main meal in themselves, depending on what you choose and the portion size. Typically you will find them listed as appetizers in restaurants but home cooks will often serve a combination of them as a main meal. Many dishes are vegetarian. Vegetables (*khoDra-waat*) are an important part of the Egyptian diet and you will find them cooked in various different ways: deep fried, with or without batter; cooked in tomato sauce; cooked in butter and served hot or cooked in olive oil and served cold.

بابا غنوج	baba ghanoush (grilled aubergine dip)
حمص	hummus
باذنجان مخلل	pickled aubergines
سلطة زبادي	yogurt and cucumber dip
ورق عنب	stuffed vine leaves
ملوخية	traditional Egyptian soup made from molokheya (a type of herb)
شوربة عدس	lentil soup
شوربة فراخ (دجاج)	chicken soup
شوربة خضار	vegetable soup

بامية	okra served in tomato sauce
كوسة محشية	stuffed courgette
كرنب محشي	stuffed cabbage leaves
مسقعة	aubergine in tomato sauce and minced lamb
زبادي	yogurt
فتوش	mixed salad tossed with pieces of toasted flatbread
خيار بالنعناع	cucumber salad with mint
تبولة	tabbouleh (bulgar wheat salad with choped vegetables, parsley and mint)
لوبية بالزيت	green beans in olive oil
فول اخضر بالزبادي	fava beans with yogurt
باذنجان مشوي	roasted aubergines
بطاطس مشوحة	sautéed potatoes
كوسة مقلية	deep-fried courgettes
قرنبيط مقلي	deep-fried cauliflower
فلافل	falafels (deep-fried spicy chickpea balls)

◆ fish

Fish is normally served grilled, roasted or tossed in flour and deep-fried. It is usually served simply, in a dressing of lemon juice and olive oil, or with tahini (a sesame seed paste).

يخنة سمك	fish stew
طاجن سمك	baked fish with vegetables
صيادية	baked fish with rice
طاجن سمك بالطحينة	fish baked in tahini sauce
كابوريا	crab
ثعابين	eel
سمك مقلي	fish fried in oil
سمك مشوي	grilled fish
استاكوزا	lobster
بوري	mullet
جمبري	prawn

FOOD AND DRINK

◆ poultry and game

Poultry and game constitute a popular element of the Egyptian diet. Pigeon, quail and duck are all enjoyed as part of Egyptian cuisine; you will, however, find that chicken is becoming more readily available and served more often in restaurants and homes.

بط بالسفرجل	roast duck with quince
شيش طاووق	chicken kebab
دجاج بالفرن	roast chicken
دجاج بالحمص	chicken with chickpeas
فتة دجاج	chicken with pieces of toasted flatbread
دجاج محشي	chicken stuffed with rice, mince and nuts
ديك رومي محشي	roast turkey with a meat and rice stuffing

◆ meat

Beef and veal remain the most widely consumed meats in Egypt, although mutton and lamb are gradually becoming more popular. The most popular way to cook meat is to grill or roast it. The word *mash-we* covers all types of meats roasted or grilled over a fire. It is the celebratory food of the Arab world, the street food, and the main fare of the restaurant trade which developed hundreds of years ago through kebab houses.

فخدة محشية	roast leg of lamb stuffed with mince, rice and nuts
شيش كباب	chunks of meat threaded onto skewers and grilled
كفتة	minced meat shaped onto skewers and grilled
كبة ضاني	minced lamb, onion and bulgur wheat
كبة نية	raw lamb, onion and bulgur wheat

كبة بالزبادي	minced lamb, onion and bulgur wheat cooked in yogurt
كبة بالصينية	meat and bulgur wheat pie served in a tray
كفتة بالحمص	meatballs with chickpeas
كفتة بالبامية	meat and okra stew
موزة عجالي بالبطاطس	veal with potatoes

◆ desserts and pastries

Throughout the Gulf lunch and dinner are usually followed by fruit. The desserts and pastries which are listed here are typically served to mark special occasions, to entertain guests or to serve with coffee and tea. Most of the desserts listed below will be available in restaurants; *baq-la-wa* and *ko-na-fa* are two of the most popular.

فواكه	fruit
خشاف بالمشمش	macerated apricots and nuts
طبق موز بالبلح	date and banana dessert
زبادي بالعسل	yogurt and honey
مهلبية	milk pudding
رز باللبن	rice pudding
بقلاوة	baklava (sweet flaky pastry topped with sweet syrup)
كنافة	shredded wheat or vermicelli pastry filled with cream
معمول	date- or nut-filled pastries
غريبة	butter biscuits
قطايف	pancakes
بسبوسة	cake made of semolina and soaked in syrup
بليلة	wheat, nuts and raisins cooked in milk and sugar
كعك	biscuits rolled in icing sugar
أم علي	filo pastry stuffed with raisins and nuts, and baked in milk

GLOSSARY OF FOOD AND DRINK

أرنب rabbit
استاكوزا lobster
أم الخلول fresh mussels
أناناس pineapple
بابا غنوج roasted aubergine
باذنجان aubergine
بامية okra
برتقال orange
برقوق plum
بسبوسة semolina cake
بصل onion
بط duckling
بطاطا sweet potatoes
بطاطس potatoes
بطيخ watermelon
بقدونس parsley
بقلاوة baklava
بلح fresh dates
بيض egg
تبولة tabbouleh
تفاح apple
تمر dates
تين fig
ثوم garlic
جبنة cheese
جزر carrot
جمبري prawn
جوزة الطيب nutmeg
حبهان cardamom
حليب milk
حلبة fenugreek
حمام baby pigeon
حمص hummus
خبز flatbread
خص lettuce
خضروات vegetables
خل vinegar

خوخ peach
خيار cucumber
ديك رومي turkey
دجاج chicken
دقيق flour
رز rice
ريحان basil
رنجة smoked mackerel
زبادي yogurt
زبدة butter
زبيب sultana
زعفران thyme
زنجبيل ginger
زيت زيتون olive oil
زيتون olive
سبانخ spinach
سحلب milk with cornflour and nuts
سردين sardines
سفرجل quince
سكر sugar
سكينة knife
سلاطة salad
سمان quail
سمك fish
سندوتش sandwich
شاي tea
شبت dill
شمام melon
شوكولاتة chocolate
صنوبر pine nuts
طبق الحلو dessert
طحينة tahini
طماطم tomatoes
عدس lentil
عسل honey
عصير juice
عنب grapes

غريبة butter shortcake
فراولة strawberry
فلفل أسمر black pepper
فلفل أخضر green pepper
فلفل أحمر red pepper
فلافل falafel
قرفة cinnamon
قرنبيط cauliflower
قطايف type of pancake
قهوة coffee
كابوريا crab
كراوية caraway drink
كرفس celery
كرنب cabbage
كركدية hibiscus
كزبرة coriander
كعك butter cake
كمثري pear
كمون cumin
كنافة shredded wheat or vermicelli dough filled with cream
كوسة courgette
لفت turnip

لحم meat
لحم بقري beef
لحم ضاني lamb
لحم عجّالي veal
لوبية خضرة green beans
لوبية ناشفة cooked dry beans
لوز almond
ليمون lemon
مربي jam
مشمش apricot
معمول pastry filled with date paste
مكرونة pasta
ملوخية green leaf broth
ملح salt
ملعقة spoon
منديل napkin
موز banana
نعناع mint leaves
هريسة semolina cake with sweet syrup
وز goose
ينسون aniseed

Nightlife in the Gulf is lively; in big cities, it is not uncommon for people to stay out late at restaurants or at venues with live music enjoying themselves until the early hours of the morning. In many restaurants you will find live music, usually traditional music, which is not necessarily advertised. In Cairo, it is not unusual for restaurants in the more upmarket areas or in the major hotels to be busy until the early hours of the morning. There are many nightclubs in Cairo, the majority of which are based in *shaa-riA al-haram* (al-haram street), although others can be found in large hotels.

Most major cities will have a variety of interesting cultural festivals, depending on the season. Information on these can be found at the tourist office or at your hotel. Local people may also be able to suggest local events and activities.

Most Egyptian males like to socialize outside the home, spending evenings in local cafes smoking shisha (flavoured tobacco), drinking tea and coffee, playing chess or backgammon, or watching a local soap opera or a football game. In these cafes alcohol is not usually served.

Cinemas are plentiful and often show up-to-date English-language movies, sometimes with Arabic subtitles. Some cinemas also show Arabic films if you feel confident enough to sit through a movie entirely in Arabic! These films sometimes have English subtitles but it is wise to check first.

The basics

band	فرقة	*fir-qa*
bar	بار	*bar*
cinema	سينما	*cinema*
club	نادي	*naa-dee*
concert	حفلة موسيقية	*Hafla moo-see-qay-ya*
dubbed film	فيلم مدبلج	*film modab-laj*
festival	مهرجان	*mihrajan*
film	فيلم	*film*
group	مجموعة	*maj-moo-Aa*

jazz	موسيقي الجاز mo-see-qa al-jaaz
musical	موسيقي moo-see-qe
opera	أوبرا opera
party	حفلة Hafla
play	مسرحية masra-Hay-ya
pop music	موسيقي البوب mo-see-qa al-pop
rock music	موسيقي الروك mo-see-qa al-rock
show	عرض AarD
subtitled film	فيلم به شريط ترجمه film be-he sha-reeT tar-jama
theatre	مسرح mas-raH
ticket	تذكرة tadh-kara
traditional music	موسيقي شعبية mo-see-qa shaA-bay-ya
to book	يحجز yaH-jiz
to go out	يخرج yakh-roj

SUGGESTIONS AND INVITATIONS

Expressing yourself

where can we go?
أين نذهب؟
ayna naz-hab?

what do you want to do?
كيف تُريد أن تقضي وقتك؟
keyfa to-reed an taq-Dee waq-tak?

what are you doing tonight?
كيف ستقضي وقتك اللَّيلة؟
keyfa sa-taq-Dee waq-tak al-lay-la?

do you have plans?
هل لديك أيّة أفكار؟
hal laday-ka ay-yat af-kaar?

would you like to ...?
هل نود أن ...
hal ta-wad an ...?

would you like to go for a coffee?

هل توجد أن نخرج انشرب قهوة؟

hal ta-wad ann nakh-roj le-nash-rab qah-wa?

we were thinking of going to ...

...كنا نفكر في الذّهاب إلى

kon-na nofak-kir fee al-dhe-haab ila ...

I can't today, but maybe some other time

لا أستطيع اليوم. لكن ربما في وقت اخر

la as-ta-TeeA al-yawm! la-kin rob-bama fee waqt aa-khar

I'm not sure I can make it

لستُ متأكد أني أستطيع عمل هذا

las-to mota-'ak-kid an-nee as-ta-TeeA Aamal ha-dha

I'd love to

بودّي عمل هذا

bo-wed-dee Aamal ha-dha

ARRANGING TO MEET

Expressing yourself

what time shall we meet?

متى نتقابل؟

mata nataqaa-bal?

where shall we meet?

أين نتقابل؟

ayna nataqaa-bal?

would it be possible to meet a bit later?

ممكن أن نلتقي متأخر قليلاً؟

mom-kin an nal-taqee mota-'akh-khir qa-lee-lan?

I have to meet ... at nine

لديّ موعد مع ... في التاسعة

laday-ya mow-Aed mAa ... fee al-taa-seAa

I don't know where it is but I'll find it on the map

لستُ أعرف هذا المكان. لكن سوف أبحث عنه على الخريطة

las-to aA-rif ha-da al-makaan, la-kin sow-fa ab-Hath An-hu Ala al-kha-ree-Ta

where should I ask the taxi driver to drop me off?

أين انزل من التاكسي؟

ayna an-zil min al-tak-see?

could you write it down for me so that I can show the driver?

مكن تكتبها لي حتى أعطيها لسائق التاكسي؟

mom-kin tak-tobha lee Hat-ta oATee-ha li-saa-'iq al-tak-see?

see you tomorrow night

أراك غداً في اللَّيل

araa-ka ghadan fee al-layl

I'll meet you later, I have to stop by the hotel first

أراك لاحقاً. يجب أن أُمِّر على الفندق أولاً

araa-ka laa-Hiqan. ya-jib ann a-morr Ala al-fon-doq aw-walan

I'll call you if there's a change of plan

سوف أتصل بك إذا تغير الموعد

sow-fa at-taSil bika/beke edha taghay-yar al-mow-Aed

are you going to eat beforehand?

هل ستأكل قبل ذلك؟

hal sa-ta'-kol qabl dha-lik?

sorry I'm late

اسف على التأخير

aa-sef/aa-sefaa Ala al-ta'-kheer

Understanding

هل هذا يُناسِبُك؟

hal ha-dha yonaa-sibak?

is that OK with you?

سامر عليك حوالي الساعة الثامنة لنذهب معا

sa'a-mor Aalay-ka Ha-waal-lee al-saa-Aa al-thaa-mina le-nadh-hab maAan

I'll come and pick you up about 8

سـوف أراك هنـاك
sow-fa araa-ka hu-nak
I'll meet you there

يـمـكـن أن نتقابل خارج ...
yom-kin an nataqaa-bal khaa-rij ...
we can meet outside …

سـأعطيك رقم هاتفي ويـمكنك الاتصال بي غدأ
sa-oA-Teek/sa-oA-Te-ke raqam haa-tifee wa yom-kinak al-it-ti-Saal bee ghadan
I'll give you my number and you can call me tomorrow

Some informal expressions

أنا مبسوط/مبسوطة ana mab-sooT/mab-soo-Ta I'm really happy
نروح نشرب ne-rooH nesh-rab to go for a drink
يأكل لُقْمَة سريعة ya'-kol loq-ma sa-ree-Aa to have a bite to eat

---

FILMS, SHOWS AND CONCERTS

Expressing yourself

is there a guide to what's on?
هل هناك كُتَيِّب عن العروض الفنِّيَّة حاليّاً؟
hal yoo-jad kotay-yib Ann al-AorooD al-fan-nay-ya Haa-le-yan?

I'd like three tickets for …
أريدُ ثلاث تذاكر ل ...
o-reed tha-laath tadhaa-kir li …

two tickets, please
تذكرتان من فضلك
tadh-kara-tayn min faD-lak

it's called …
اسمه ...
is-moh …

what time does it start?
متي يبدأ العرض؟
mata yab-da' al-AarD?

are you sure there are subtitles?
هل انت متأكد ان العرض به شريط ترجمة؟
hal an-ta mota'ak-kid an-na al-AarD be-he sha-reeT tar-jama?

I'd like to go and see a show
أريدُ الذّهاب لمشاهدة عرض فني
o-reed al-dhe-haab le-mosha-hadat AarD fan-nee

how long is it on for?
كم مدة بقاءعرضه؟
kam mod-dat ba-qa' Aar-Do?

are there tickets for another day?
هل يوجد تذاكر في يوم اخر؟
hal yoo-jad tadhaa-kir fee yawm aa-khar?

are there any free concerts?
هل يوجد حفلات موسيقية مجّانية؟
hal yoo-jad Haf-laat moo-see-qay-ya maj-jaa-nay-ya?

what sort of music is it?
ما نوع هذه الموسيقى؟
maa nooA ha-dhe-he al-moo-see-qa?

it would be nice to see some traditional music
أحب مشاهدة موسيقى الفنون الشعبية
oHib moshaa-hadat moo-see-qa al-fu-noon al-shaA-bay-ya

Understanding

إنّها حفلة موسيقية في مكان مكشوف
in-naha Haf-la mo-see-qay-a fee makaan mak-shoof
it's an open-air concert

لقد نالت إعجاب الكثير من المشاهدين
laqad naa-lat iA-jaab al-ka-theer min al-mosha-hideen
it's had very good reviews

سوف تُعرَض الأسبوع القادم
sow-fa toA-raD al-os-booA al-qaa-dim
it comes out next week

لقد نُفذت كل تذاكر هذا العرض
laqad nafadhat koll tadhaa-kir ha-dha al-AarD
that showing's sold out

كل التذاكر محجوزة حتى ...
koll al-tadhaa-kir maH-jooza Hat-ta ...
it's all booked up until ...

لا يجب الحجز مسبَّقاً
laa ya-jib al-Hajz mos-baqan
there's no need to book in advance

رجاء إغلاق التليفونات المحمولة
rajaa' igh-laaq al-tele-foo-naat al-maH-moo-la
please turn off your mobile phones

لا يوجد حجز مقاعد
laa yoo-jad Hajz maqaa-Aed
there is no assigned seating

هذه فرقة مشهورة جداً
ha-dhe-he firqa mash-hoo-ra jid-dan
this is a very popular group

هو مغنٍّ مشهور جداً / هي مغنّية مشهورة جداً
hu-wa mo-ghan-nee mash-hoor jid-dan/he-ya moghan-neya mash-hoora
   jid-dan
he/she is a famous singer

PARTIES AND CLUBS

Expressing yourself

I'm having a little leaving party tonight
لديّ حفلة وَداع صغيرة اللّيلة
laday-ya Haf-lat wadaA Sa-ghee-ra al-lay-la

should I bring something to drink?

هل أُحضر معي بعض المشروبات؟

hal oH-Dir ma-Aee baAD al-mash-roo-baat

are there any clubs where we can go dancing?

هل يوجد نوادي ليلية نرقص فيها؟

hal yoo-jad nawaa-dee lay-lay-ya nar-qoS fee-ha?

we could go to a club afterwards

ممكن نروح إلى أحد النوادي الليلية بعد ذلك

mom-kin ne-rooH ila aHad al-nawaa-dee al-lay-lay-ya baAD dha-lik

do you have to pay to get in?

هل هناك رسم دخول؟

hal hu-nak rasm do-khool?

I have to meet someone inside

لدي موعد بالداخل

laday-ya mow-Aed bel-daa-khil

will you let me back in when I come back?

هل سَيُسمح لي بالدخول مرة ثانية عند العودة؟

hal sa-yos-maH lee bel-do-khool mar-ra tha-ne-ya Aen-da al-Aow-da?

the DJ's really cool

مشغّل الإسطوانات ممتاز

moshagh-ghil al-os-To-waa-naat mum-taaz

I like the mix of Arabic and Western music

أحب خلط الموسيقى العربية مع الموسيقى الغربية

oHib khalT al-moo-see-qa al-Aara-bay-ya maAa al-moo-see-qa al-ghar-bay-ya

thanks, but I'm with my boyfriend

شكراً. أنا هنا مع صديقي / صديقتي

shok-ran. ana hu-na mAa Sa-dee-qee/Sa-dee-qatee

no thanks, I don't smoke

لا. شكراً. أنا لا أُدخّن

laa. shok-ran. ana la odakh-khin

Understanding

هناك حفلة في منزل هاني
hu-nak Hafla fee man-zil hany
there's a party at Hany's place

هل تحب / تحبين الرقص؟
hal to-Hib/to-Hib-een al-raqS?
do you want to dance?

هل أشتري لك مشروب؟
hal ash-taree laka/lakee mash-roob?
can I buy you a drink?

هل معك كبريت؟
hal maAak kab-reet?
have you got a light?

هل معك كبريت؟
hal maAak kab-reet?
have you got a cigarette?

هل ممكن أن نتقابل مرة أخرى؟
mom-kin nataqaa-bal mar-ra okh-ra?
can we see each other again?

ممكن أوصلك للبيت؟
mom-kin owaS-Salik lil-bayt?
can I see you home?

TOURISM AND SIGHTSEEING

There are many magnificent tourist attractions in the Gulf region, from the legendary Pyramids at Giza to less well-known but equally impressive monuments, ruins and classical as well as contemporary architecture. Any tourist office will be able to give you information on monuments and sites, costs and opening hours; sometimes, however, talking to locals is just as valuable, as they will be able to direct you to interesting and less well-known sites of interest which have much to offer.

Admission prices to museums in Egypt are very reasonable. The Egyptian Museum (al-mat-Haf al-maS-ree) in Cairo, established in 1853 and now based in a state-of-the-art neo-classical style building designed by the French architect Marcel Dourgnon, exhibits a huge collection now exceeding 120,000 artefacts ranging from the pre-historic era to the Greco-Roman period.

Transportation to and from attractions should be relatively easy; most bus or taxi terminals will run services to the major sites, which may be a more convenient way to travel. You may also want to consider hiring a personal taxi for the day; the driver will agree a price with you in advance and then take you on the itinerary of your choice.

The basics

ancient	أثري	atharee
antique	أثر	athar
area	منْطقة	man-Tiqa
bazaar	بازار	bazaar
century	قرن	qarn
church	كنيسة	kanee-sa
exhibition	معرض	maA-raD
gallery	معرض	maA-raD
modern art	فن حديث	fan Ha-deeth

mosque	مسجد *mas-jid*
museum	متحف *mat-Haf*
painting	لوحة زيتية *low-Ha zay-tay-ya*
park	حديقة *Ha-dee-qa*
pharaoh	فرعون *fir-Aoon*
Pyramids	اهرامات *ahraa-maat*
ruins	أطلال *aT-laal*
sculpture	نموذج فني *namoo-zaj fan-nee*
sphinx	أبو الهول *abu al-hool*
statue	تمثال *tim-thal*
street map	خريطة الشوارع *kha-ree-Tat al-shawa-riA*
tour guide	مُرشد *mor-shid*
tourist	سائح *sa-'eH*
tourist information centre	مركز الإرشاد السياحي *mar-kaz al-ir-shhad al-se-yaa-Hee*
town centre	وسط البلد *wasaT al-balad*

Expressing yourself

I'd like some information on …
… أريد بعض المعلومات عن
o-reed baAD al-maA-loo-maat Aan …

can you tell me where the tourist information centre is?
ممكن تدلني أين أجد مركز الإرشاد السياحي؟
mon-kin ta-dol-lanee ayna ajid mar-kaz al-ir-shaad al-se-yaa-Hee?

do you have a street map of the town?
هل لديك خريطة لشوارع المدينة؟
hal laday-ka kha-ree-Ta le-shawa-riA al-ma-dee-na?

I was told there's an ancient mosque we can visit
سمعت أن هناك مسجد أثري يمكننا زيارته
sa-miAto an-na hu-naak mas-jid atharee yom-kinona ze-yaa-ratoh

can you show me where it is on the map?
ممكن أن تدلني أين هذا المكان على الخريطة؟
mom-kin ann ta-dol-lanee ayna ha-dha al-makaan Aala al-kha-ree-Ta?

how do you get there?
كيف تصل إلى هذا المكان؟
keyfa ta-Sil ila ha-dha al-makaan?

is it free?
هل الدُّخول مجاني؟
hal al-do-khool maj-jaa-nee?

when was it built?
متى بُنِيَ هذا المكان؟
mata boneya ha-dha al-makaan?

Understanding

رسم دُخول	admission
مُغلق	closed
حرب	war
غزوٌ	invasion
مفتوح	open
تجديد	renovation
أعمال ترميم	restoration work
جولة مع مرشد	guided tour
أنت الآن موجود هنا	you are here *(on a map)*

يجب عليك أَن تسأل حين تصل الى المكان
ya-jib Aalay-ka an tas-'al Hee-na taSil ila al-makaan
you'll have to ask when you get there

ستبدأ الجولة مع مرشد السَّاعة الثَّانية
satab-da' al-jow-la mAa mor-shid al-saa-Aa al-thaa-ne-ya
the next guided tour starts at 2 o'clock

MUSEUMS, EXHIBITIONS AND MONUMENTS

Expressing yourself

I've heard there's a very good exhibition on at the moment
سَمِعتُ أَنَّ هناك معرض جميل يُعرَض الآن
sa-miA-tu an-na hu-naak maA-raD ja-meel yoA-raD al-aan

how much is it to get in?
كَم سِعر الدُّخول؟
kam siAr al-do-khool

is this ticket valid for the exhibition as well?

هل هذه التذكرة صالحة لدخول المعرض أيضاً؟

hal ha-dh-he al-tadh-kara Saa-liHa li-do-khool al-maA-raD ay-Dan?

are there any discounts for young people?

هل هناك تذاكر مخفَّضة للشباب؟

hal yoo-jad tadhaa-kir mokhaf-faDa lil-sha-baab?

is it open on Sundays?

هل هو مفتوح أيّام الأحد؟

hal hu-wa maf-tooH ay-yaam al-aHad?

two concessions and one full price, please

تذكرتين مخفَّضتين وواحدة كاملة من فضلك

tadhkara-tayn mokhaf-faDa-tayn wa waa-Hida kaa-mila min faD-lak

I have a student card

معى كارت طلبة

ma-Aee kart Talaba

Understanding

مكتب التَّذاكر	ticket office
معرض مؤقّت	temporary exhibition
معرض دائم	permanent exhibition
ممنوع استخدام فلاش التصوير	no flash photography
ممنوع التصوير	no photography
هذا الإتجاه	this way
الرجا التزام الهدوء	silence, please
من فضلك، ممنوع لمس المعروضات	please do not touch

سعر دخول المتحف ...

siAr do-khool al-mat-Haf ...

admission to the museum costs ...

هذه التذكرة تسمح لك بدخول المعرض

ha-dhe-he al-tadh-kara tas-maH laka be-do-khool al-maA-raD

this ticket also allows you access to the exhibition

GIVING YOUR IMPRESSIONS

Expressing yourself

it's beautiful
إنّها جميلة
in-naha ja-mee-la

it was beautiful
كانت جميلة
kaa-nat ja-mee-la

it's fantastic
إنّها رائعة
in-naha raa-'e-Aa

it was fantastic
كانت رائعة
kaa-nat raa-'e-Aa

I really enjoyed it
استمتعتُ بها
is-tam-taA-tu bi-ha

I didn't like it that much
لم تعجبني كثيرا
lam toA-jib-nee ka-thee-ran

it was a bit boring
كان ملّ بعضَ الشيء
kaa-na mo-mill baAD al-shay'

it's expensive for what it is
إنها غالية بالنسبة لقيمتها
in-naha ghaa-laya bil-nisba li-qee-mataha

it's very touristy
أنها سياحية جداً
in-naha see-ya-Hey-ya jid-dan

it was really crowded
كانت مزدحمة جداً
kaa-nat moz-dattima jid-dan

we didn't go in the end, the queue was too long

لم نتمكن من الدخول لأن الطابور كان طويل

lam natamak-kan min al-do-khool li-'an-na al-Ta-boor kaa-na Ta-weel

we didn't have time to see everything

لم يكن لدينا وقت كاف لرؤية كل شيئ

lam yakon laday-na waqt kaa-fee li-ro'-yat kol shay'

Understanding

مشهور	famous
يستحق التصوير	picturesque
نموذج معبّر عن	typical
تقليدي	traditional

لا تدع الفرصة تفوتك لمشاهدة ...

laa tadaA/laa-tada-Aee al-for-Sa ta-foo-tak / ta-foo-tik li-moshaa-hadat ...

you really must go and see ...

أنا أرشّح لك الذهاب إلى ...

ana o-rash-shiH laka al-dhe-haab ila ...

I recommend going to ...

هناك منظر رائع يُطلّ على المدينة بالكامل

hu-naak man-Zar ra-'eA yo-Till Ala al-ma-dee-na bil-kaa-mil

there's a wonderful view over the whole city

أصبح سياحي إلى حد كبير

aS-baHa see-ya-Hee ila Hadd ka-beer

it's become a bit too touristy

انهدم الساحل تماماً

in-hadama al-sa-Hil tamaa-man

the coast has been completely ruined

SPORTS AND GAMES

Given the vast geography and landscape of the Arabic-speaking world you can find almost any type of sporting activity. Even Lebanon has world-class ski slopes in the northern part of the country and Dubai can boast one of the largest indoor ski slopes in the world, should you feel like skiing after spending a few hours in the sweltering heat.

The natural landscape provides for great hikes and treks, particularly given the mountainous geography. In Egypt, the Sinai rock mountains are fast becoming a destination for trekkers. Many countries have picked up on this and now offer guided tours and expeditions. Information on the steadily increasing number of hiking and walking paths should be available at the local tourist office or any travel agency.

The countries on the Mediterranean offer tourists good surfing and other water sports. Swimming and diving are popular, particularly around the coral reefs off the Red Sea and the coast of Sinai.

Probably the most popular sport among locals, as in almost all parts of the world, is football. Various card games and board games such as backgammon are also widely played.

The basics

ball	كرة	korah
basketball	كرة سلة	korat sal-la
board game	العاب الواح التسالي	al-Aaab al-waaH al-tasaa-lee
cards	لعب الورق	loAbat al-waraq (kot-she-na)
chess	شطرنج	shaTa-ranj
cycling	ركوب الدراجات	rokoob al-dar-ra-jaat
football	كرة القدم	korat al-qadam
hiking path	درب رحلات السير	darb riH-lat al-sayr
match	ماتش	match

mountain biking	صعود الجبال بالدراجات So-Aood al-ji-baal bil-dar-ra-jaat
sport	رياضة re-yaa-Da
surfing	رياضة ركوب الأمواج re-yaa-Dat rokoob al-am-waaj
swimming	سباحة se-baa-Ha
swimming pool	حمام سباحة Ham-maam se-baa-Ha
table football	كرة قدم الطاولة korat qadam al-Tow-la
tennis	تنس tennis
trip	رحلة riHla
to go hiking	يخرج في رحلة سير yokh-roj fee riHlat sayr
to have a game of ...	يلعب لعبة... yal-Aab loA-bat ...
to play	يلعب yal-Aab

Expressing yourself

I'd like to hire ... for an hour
أريد إستئجار ... لمدة ساعة
o-reed is-ti'-jaar ...li-mod-dat saa-Aa

are there ... lessons available?
هل يوجد دروس تعليم ...؟
hal yoo-jad do-roos taA-leem ...?

how much is it per person per hour?
كم يتكلف ذلك للشخص في الساعة؟
kam yatakal-laf dha-lik lil-shakhS fee al-saa-Aa?

I'm not very sporty
لست من هواة الرياضة
las-to min ho-waat al-re-yaa-Da

I've never done it before
لم اقم بذلك من قبل
lam aqom bi-dha-lik min qabl

I've done it once or twice, a long time ago
مارست هذا مرة أو مرتين منذ وقت طويل
maa-ras-to ha-dha mar-ra aw mar-ra-tayn mon-dho waqt Ta-weel

I'm exhausted!
أنا تعبان
ana taA-baan

SPORTS AND GAMES

I'd like to go and watch a football match
أريد الذهاب لمشاهدة مباراة كرة قدم
o-reed al-dhe-haab li-moshaa-hadat mobaa-raat kort qadam

shall we stop for a picnic?
هل ممكن أن نتوقف قليلاً للإستراحة وتناول الطعام؟
hal mom-kin an natawaq-qaf qa-lee-lan lil-is-tiraa-Ha wa tanaa-wol al-Ta-Aaam?

we played ...
لعبنا ...
la-Aib-na ...

Understanding

... للإيجار   ... for hire

هل مارست هذا من قبل أم أنت مبتدئ؟
hal ma-rast ha-dha min qabl am an-ta mub-ta-di'?
do you have any experience, or are you a complete beginner?

يجب دفع تأمين إيجار قدره ...
ya-jib dafA ta'-meen ee-jaar qad-ro ...
there is a deposit of ...

HIKING

Expressing yourself

are there any hiking paths around here?
هل يوجد دروب لرحلات السير علي الأقدام هنا؟
hal yoo-jad do-roob li-reH-laat al-sayr Ala al-aqdam hu-na?

can you recommend any good walks in the area?
هل تقترح طرق جيدة للسير في هذه الناحية؟
hal taq-tariH Toroq jay-yi-da lil-sayr fee ha-dhe-he al-na-Hiya?

I've heard there's a nice walk by the lake
سمعت أن هناك طريق ممتع للسير بالقرب من البحيرة
sa-meAto an-na hu-nak Ta-reeq mom-tiA lil-sayr bil-qorb min al-bo-Hay-ra

we're looking for a short walk somewhere round here

نريد الذهاب للتنزه في جولة قصيرة بالقرب من هنا

no-reed al-dhe-haab lil-tanaz-zoh fee jow-la qaSee-ra bil-qorb min hu-na

can I hire hiking boots?

هل يمكن استئجار أحذية مناسبة لرحلات السير؟

hal yom-kin is-ti'-jaar aH-dhiya monaa-siba li-reH-laat al-sayr?

how long does the hike take?

ما مدّة رحلة السير؟

maa mod-dat riHlat al-sayr?

is it very steep?

هل هو شديد الإنحدار؟

hal hu-wa sha-deed al-in-Hi-daar?

where's the start of the path?

أين بداية الدرب؟

ayna be-daa-yat al-darb?

is the path waymarked?

هل الدرب به علامات إرشادية؟

hal al-darb be-he Aalaa-maat ir-shaa-day-ya?

is it a circular path?

هل الدرب دائري؟

hal al-darb daa-'e-ree

Understanding

المدّة التقديرية   average duration *(of walk)*

تستغرق حوالي ثلاث ساعات ونصف بما في ذلك فترة الإستراحة

tas-tagh-riq Ha-waa-lee tha-laath saa-Aaat wa nesf bi-ma fee dha-lik fat-rat al-is-ti-raa-Ha

it's about a three-hour walk including rest stops

أحضر معطف ضد البلل وأحذية مريحة للسير

aH-Dir miA-Taf Did al-balal wa aH-dhiya moree-Ha lil-sayr

bring a waterproof jacket and some walking shoes

OTHER SPORTS

Expressing yourself

where can we hire bikes?
أين يمكن إستئجار درّاجات؟
ayna yom-kin is-ti'-jaar dar-ra-jaat?

are there any cycle paths?
هل يوجد دروب لسير الدرّاجات؟
hal yoo-jad do-roob li-sayr al-dar-ra-jaat?

does anyone have a football?
هل يوجد أحد لديه كرة قدم؟
hal yoo-jad aHad laday-he ko-rat qadam?

which team do you support?
أي فريق تشجع؟
ayy fareeq toshaj-jiA?

I support ...
أنا أشجع ...
ana o-shaj-jiA …

is there an open-air swimming pool?
هل يوجد حمّام سباحة مكشوف هنا؟
hal yoo-jad Ham-maam se-baa-Ha mak-shoof hu-na?

I've never been diving before
لم يسبق لي ممارسة رياضة الغطس من قبل
lam yas-biq lee mo-maa-rasat re-yaa-Dat al-ghaTs min qabl

I run for half an hour every morning
أمارس رياضة العدو لمدة نصف ساعة كل صباح
o-maa-ris re-yaa-Dat al-Aadoo li-mod-dat neSf saa-Aa kol Sa-baH

Understanding

يوجد ملعب تنس للإستخدام العام ليس بعيداً عن المحطة
yoo-jad mal-Aab tennis lil-is-tikh-dam al-Aaam lay-sa baAeed Aan al-ma-HaT-Ta

there's a public tennis court not far from the station

ملعب التنس مشغول الآن
mal-Aab al-tennis mash-ghool al-aan
the tennis court's occupied

هل تستطيع السباحة؟
Hal tas-ta-TeeA al-se-baa-Ha?
can you swim?

هل تلعب كرة سلَّة؟
hal tal-Aab korat sal-la?
do you play basketball?

INDOOR GAMES

Expressing yourself

shall we have a game of cards?

هل نلعب الورق؟
hal nal-Aab al-waraq (kot-she-na)?

does anyone know any good card games?

هل يعرف أحدكم لعبة ورق جيدة؟
hal yaA-rif aHa-dokom loA-bat waraq jay-ye-da?

it's your turn

هذا دورك
ha-dha dow-rak

Understanding

هل تستطيع لعب الشطرغ؟
hal tas-ta-TeeA liAb al-shaTa-ranj?
do you know how to play chess?

هل معك كوتشينة؟
hal ma-Aa-ak kot-she-na?
do you have a pack of cards?

Some informal expressions

كش ملك! *kish malik!* check to the king!

المتش حيبتدي إمتي؟ *al-match Ha-yib-tedee im-ta?* what time does the match start?

هو غلبني *hu-wa ghala-banee* he thrashed me

لعبة مملة *loA-ba moo-mila* that was a boring game

Most shops are closed on Fridays, although in countries with sizeable Christian populations, including Lebanon, Syria, Jordan and Egypt, some shops open on Fridays but close on Sundays. Egypt is a shopper's paradise, and you will be in luck whether you are looking for a kitsch Pharaoh souvenir, hand-embroidered cloths or bedouin scarves.

Most large shopping malls and complexes will have set opening hours, usually between 9am and 9pm, but this varies according to the season and according to each mall. However, if you are doing your shopping in the many *souqs* (markets) throughout the Arab world, you will find that their hours (and prices!) are much more flexible. It is not uncommon to stroll through the famous labyrinthine Khan al-khalee-lee Market in Cairo close to midnight and still find vendors open. Markets such as this are found in almost all cities, big and small, throughout the Arabic-speaking world. Here you can buy anything from a souvenir postcard to an antique backgammon table.

In the markets you will find it difficult to pay by credit card and debit cards are not used at all, so you should remember to carry sufficient cash. Prices in markets are typically not fixed, so you should try to bargain for anything you want to buy; indeed, haggling is expected although you should remember that it is very bad form to engage in haggling and then refuse to buy the item at all. At malls payment by credit card is much easier. If you pay in cash, some countries allow you to pay in either the local currency, American dollars or euros.

Cigarettes can be bought at almost any confectionery store or from street vendors. Alcohol is not as difficult to come by as you might expect, but there are no recognizable off-licences that stay open late. You will have to ask around, but most supermarkets carry alcohol. In countries such as Lebanon, alcohol is easy to find in confectionery stores. Gifts are not usually wrapped so you shouldn't expect a salesperson to offer this service.

The basics

bakery	مخبز	makh-baz
butcher's	جزار	jaz-zar
cash desk	الخزينة	al-kha-zee-na
cheap	رخيص	ra-kheeS
checkout	دفع قيمة المشتروات	dafA qee-mat al-mosh-tarawaat
clothes	ملابس	malaa-bis
expensive	غالي	gha-lee
gram	جرام	gram
greengrocer's	محل خضروات	maHal khoDra-waat
kilo	كيلو	kee-loo
present	هدية	ha-day-ya
price	سعر	siAr
receipt	إيصال	ee-Saal
refund	استرداد النقود	is-tir-dad al-no-qood
sales assistant	بائع	ba-'eA
sales	بضاعة مخفّضة	beDaaAa mokhaf-faDa
shop	محل	maHal
shopping centre	مركز تسوق	mar-kaz tasow-woq
souvenir	هدية تذكارية	ha-day-ya tidhka-ray-ya
supermarket	سوبر ماركت	so-ber market
to buy	يشتري	yash-taree
to cost	يكلف	yo-kal-lif
to pay	يدفع	yad-faA
to sell	يبيع	ya-beeA

SHOPPING

Expressing yourself

is there a supermarket near here?
هل يوجد سوبر ماركت قريب من هنا؟
hal yoo-jad so-ber market qa-reeb min hu-na?

where can I buy cigarettes?
أين يمكن شراء سجائر؟
ayna yom-kin she-raa' sa-gaa-'ir?

I'd like ...
... أريد
o-reed ...

I'm looking for ...
... أنا أبحث عن
ana ab-Hath Aan ...

do you sell ...?
... هل تبيع؟
hal ta-beeA ...

do you know where I might find some ...?
هل تعرف أين يمكن أن أجد ...؟
hal taA-rif ayna yom-kin an ajid ...?

can you order it for me?
ممكن تطلبها لي؟
mom-kin toT-lob-ha lee?

how much is this?
كم سعر هذا؟
kam siAr ha-dha?

I'll take it
سوف آخذ هذا
sow-fa a-khod ha-dha

I haven't got much money
ليس معي نقود كثيرة
lay-sa ma-Ae noqood ka-thee-ra

I haven't got enough money

ليس لدي نقود كافية
lay-sa laday-ya noqood kaa-feya

that's everything, thanks

هذا كل شيء. شكرا
ha-dha kol shay', shok-ran

can I have a (plastic) bag?

ممكن تعطيني شنطة بلاستيك؟
mom-kin taA-Tee-nee shan-Ta bilas-tik?

I think you've made a mistake with my change

هناك خطأ في حساب باقي النقود
hu-naak khaTa' fee Hi-saab baa-qee al-noqood

Understanding

مفتوح من ... حتى ...	open from … to …
يغلق أيام الأحد من الواحدة حتى الثالثة ظهرا	closed Sundays/1pm to 3pm
عرض خاص	special offer
بضائع مخفضة	sales

هل هناك أي شيء أخر؟
hal hu-naak ay shay' aa-khar?
will there be anything else?

هل تريد شنطة؟
hal to-reed shan-Ta?
would you like a bag?

PAYING

Expressing yourself

where do I pay?

أين أدفع؟
ayna ad-faA?

how much do I owe you?

كم يجب أن أدفع؟

kam ya-jib ann ad-fA?

could you write it down for me, please?

ممكن تكتبها لى من فضلك؟

mom-kin tak-tob-ha lee min faD-lak?

can I pay by credit card?

ممكن أدفع ببطاقة الإئتمان؟

mom-kin ad-faA bi-be-Ta-qat al-'e-ti-man?

I'll pay in cash

سوف أدفع نقدا

sow-fa ad-faA naq-dan

I'm sorry, I haven't got any change

أنا آسف. ليس لدى أى فكّه

ana aa-sef. lay-sa laday-ya fak-ka

can I have a receipt?

ممكن تديني إيصال؟

mom-kin ted-dee-nee ee-Saal?

Understanding

ادفع عند الخزينة

id-fAa Aen-da al-kha-zee-na

pay at the cash desk

كيف تريد أن تدفع؟

keyfa to-reed an tad-faA?

how would you like to pay?

هل لديك أقل من ذلك؟

ha laday-ka aqall min dha-lik?

do you have anything smaller?

هل لديك إثبات شخصية؟

hal laday-ka ith-baat shakh-Say-ya?

have you got any ID?

من فضلك! قم بالتوقيع هنا
min faD-lak! qom bil-tow-qeeA hu-na?
could you sign here, please?

FOOD

Expressing yourself

where can I buy food around here?
أين يمكن شراء طعام بالقرب من هنا؟
ayna yom-kin she-raa' Ta-Aaam bil-qorb min hu-na?

is there a market?
هل يوجد سوق هنا؟
hal yoo-jad sooq hu-na?

is there a bakery around here?
هل يوجد مخبز بالقرب من هنا؟
hal yoo-jad makh-baz bil-qorb min hu-na?

it's for four people
إنه لأربعة أشخاص
in-naho li-ar-baAat ash-khaS

about 300 grams
حوالى ثلاثمائة جرام
Ha-waa-lee tha-laath me-'at gram

a kilo of apples, please
كيلو تفاح من فضلك
kee-loo tif-faaH min faD-lak

a bit less/more
أقل قليلاً / أكثر
aqall qa-lee-lan/ak-thar

can I taste it?
يمكن أتذوقه؟
mom-kin atadhow-waqo?

does it travel well?
هل يمكن السفر به مسافة طويلة؟
hal yom-kin al-sa-far be-he masaa-fa Ta-wee-la?

Understanding

أصناف محلية ذات طعم خاص	local specialities
مصنوع من مواد عضوية	organic
مصنوع في البيت	homemade
ينصح بإستخدامه قبل ...	best before ...
محل لبيع الوجبات الخاصة	delicatessen

هناك سوق كل يوم حتى الواحدة ظهرا
hu-naak sooq kol yawm Hat-ta al-waa-Hida Zoh-ran
there's a market every day until 1pm

يوجد محل خضروات قريب من هنا يفتح حتى وقت متأخر
yoo-jad maHal khoDra-waat qa-reeb min hu-na yaf-taH Hat-ta waqt mota-akh-khir
there's a grocer's just on the corner that's open late

CLOTHES

Expressing yourself

I'm looking for the menswear section
أنا أبحث عن القسم الرجالي
ana ab-Hath Ann al-qism al-re-jaa-lee

no thanks, I'm just looking
لا،شكرا. إنني اخذ فكرة فقط
laa, shok-ran. in-na-nee aa-khod fikra faqaT

can I try it on?
ممكن أقيسه؟
mom-kin a-qee-soh?

I'd like to try the one in the window
ممكن أقيس الذي في نافذة العرض؟
mom-kin a-qees al-la-dhee fee na-fidhat al-AarD?

I take a size 39 (in shoes)
أنا أرتدي مقاس تسعة وثلاثون
ana ar-tadee maqaas tis-Aa wa thalaa-thoon

where are the changing rooms?
أين غرف قياس الملابس؟
ayna ghor-fat qe-yaas al-malaa-bis?

it doesn't fit
هذا لايناسبني
ha-dha la yona-sib-nee

it's too big/small
إنه كبير / صغير جدا
in-naho ka-beer/Sa-gheer jid-dan

do you have it in another colour?
هل يوجد هذا الموديل بلون آخر
hal yoo-jad ha-dha al-mo-dayl be-lown aa-khar?

do you have it in a smaller/bigger size?
هل يوجد نفس الموديل بمقاس أصغر أو أكبر؟
hal yoo-jad nafs al-mo-dayl be-ma-qaas aS-ghar aw ak-bar?

do you have them in red?
هل لديك هذه الموديلات بلون أحمر؟
hal laday-ka ha-dhe-he al-moo-dil-laat be-loon aH-mar?

yes, that's fine, I'll take them
حسناً. سأشتريهم
Hasa-nan. sa'shta-reehom

no, I don't like it
لا. لأأريده
laa, laa o-ree-doh

I'll think about it
أحتاج بعض الوقت للتفكير
aH-taaj baAD al-waqt lil-taf-keer

I'd like to return this, it doesn't fit
أريد رد هذا. إنه لايناسبني
o-reed radd ha-dha. in-naho laa yoo-na-sib-nee

this ... has a hole in it, can I get a refund?

هذا ... به ثقب. هل يمكن إعادته و استرداد النقود؟

ha-dha…be-he thoqb. hal mom-kin eAaa-datih wa-is-tir-dad al-noqood?

Understanding

غرف قياس الملابس	changing rooms
البضاعة المخفضة لايمكن ترجيعها	sale items cannot be returned
مفتوح أيام الأحد	open Sunday
ملابس أطفال	children's clothes
ملابس نسائية (حريمى)	ladieswear
ملابس رجالى	menswear
ملابس حريمى داخلية	lingerie

مرحبا. يمكن أساعدك؟

mar-Haba, mom-kin osaa-Aedak?

hello, can I help you?

ليس لدينا إلا اللون الأزرق أوالأسود

lay-sa laday-na il-la al-lown al-az-raq aw al-as-wad

we only have it in blue or black

لم يبقى شيئ من هذا المقاس

lam yab-qa shay' min ha-dha al-ma-qaas

we don't have any left in that size

إنه يناسبك

in-naho yonaa-si-bak/yo-naa-si-bik

it suits you

إنه مناسب تماما

in-na-ho mona-sib tamaa-man

it's a good fit

يمكن رده إذا لم يكن مناسب

mom-kin rad-do idha lam yakon mona-sib

you can bring it back if it doesn't fit

SOUVENIRS AND PRESENTS

Expressing yourself

I'm looking for a present to take home

أنا أبحث عن هدية آخذها معى الي بلدي

ana ab-Hath Aan ha-day-ya aa-khodh-ha ma-Aee ila baladee

I'd like something that's easy to transport

أريد شيئا يسهل حمله فى السفر

o-reed shay-' yas-hol Ham-lo fee al-safar

it's for a little girl of four

أنه لفتاة عمرها أربع سنوات

in-naho li-fa-tah Aom-raha ar-baA sanawaat

Understanding

مصنوع من الخشب / الفضة/ الذهب / الصوف	made of wood/silver/gold/wool
مصنوع يدويا	handmade
منتج تقليدى مصنوع يدويا	traditionally made product

كم تريد أن تنفق؟

kam to-reed an ton-fiq?

how much do you want to spend?

هل هذا من أجل هدية؟

hal ha-dha min ajl ha-day-ya?

is it for a present?

هذا المنتج خاص من هذه المنطقة

ha-dha al-mon-taj khaaS min ha-dhe-he al-man-Ti-qa

it's typical of the region

PHOTOS

You will no doubt come across some amazing and wonderful sights during your travels, but there are a few things to remember when taking photos of people. As a matter of courtesy, you should always ask the permission of the person you are photographing. Be respectful of the fact that the person may not want to be photographed or may not consider what they are doing to be worth photographing. You should also avoid taking any pictures of or near military bases or installations; if you do your camera may be confiscated. If you want to take pictures of government offices be sure to obtain permission from someone working in the building.

The cost of developing photos is significantly cheaper in the Gulf than in the UK. Photo shops will often print pictures straight from your memory card; alternatively you can download pictures and burn them to CD at most Internet cafés.

The basics

black and white	ابيض واسود *ab-yaD wa as-wad*
camera	كاميرا *kamera*
colour	ملوّن *mo-low-wan*
CD	سي دي *see-dee*
copy	نسخة *nos-kha*
digital camera	كاميرا رقمية *kamera raqmay-ya*
disposable camera	كاميراللإستخدام مرة واحدة *kamera lil-is-tikh-dam mar-ra waa-Hida*
exposure	لقطة *laq-Ta*
film	فيلم *film*
flash	فلاش *flash*
glossy	لاميع *lam-meeA*
matte	مطّ *maTT*
memory card	كارت الذاكرة *kart al-zaa-ki-ra*
negative	نيجاتيف *neja-teef*
passport photo	صور للباسبور *So-war lil-bas-boor*

photo booth	كشك تصوير شخصي *koshk taS-weer shakh-See*
reprint	نسخة *nos-kha*
slide	مجموعة صور متتالية *maj-moo-Aat So-war mota-taa-laya*
to get photos developed	يحمّض الصُّور *yoo-Ham-miD al-So-war*
to take a photo/photos	يلتقط صورة / صور *yal-taqiT Soo-ra/So-war*

Expressing yourself

could you take a photo of us, please?
ممكن تلتقط لنا صورة من فضلك؟
mom-kin tal-taqiT lana Soo-ra min faD-lak?

you just have to press this button
اضغط علي هذا الزّر
eD-ghaT Ala ha-dha al-zir

I'd like a colour film
أريد فيلم ألوان
o-reed film al-waan

do you have black and white films?
هل يوجد أفلام أبيض وأسود؟
hal yoo-jad af-lam ab-yaD wa as-wad?

how much is it to develop a film of 36 photos?
كم يكلف تحميض فيلم36 صورة؟
kam youkal-lif taH-meeD film sit-ta wa thala-thoon Soo-ra?

I'd like to have this film developed
أريد تحميض هذا الفيلم
o-reed taH-meeD ha-dha al-film

I'd like extra copies of some of the photos
أريد نسخ إضافية من بعض الصور
o-reed no-sakh iDaa-fay-ya min baAD al So-war

three copies of this one and two of this one
ثلاثة نسخ من هذه ونسختان من هذه
thalaa-that nosakh min ha-dhe-he wa noskha-tayn min ha-dh-he

can I print my digital photos here?
هل يمكن طباعة الصُّور الرقميَّة هنا؟
hal yom-kin TibaaAat al-So-war al-raqa-may-ya hu-na?

can you put these photos on a CD for me?
هل يمكن وضع نسخة من الصور علي سي دي؟
hal yom-kin waDA nos-kha min al-So-war Ala see-dee?

I've come to pick up my photos
أريد الحصول علي صوري
o-reed al-HoSool Ala Sowa-ree

I've got a problem with my camera
يوجد عطل بالكاميرا
yoo-jad AoTl bil-kamera

I don't know what it is
لا أدري ما هو
laa aA-rif maa hu-wa

the flash doesn't work
الفلاش لا يعمل
al-flash laa yaA-mal

Understanding

تحميض الصُّور في خلال ساعة	photos developed in one hour
خدمة سريعة	express service
طبع الصُّور علي سي دي	photos on CD

رما تكون البطَّارية فاضية
rob-bama ta-koon al-baT-Ta-ray-ya faD-ya
maybe the battery's dead

لدينا جهاز لطبع الصُّور الرقميَّة
laday-na ji-haaz li-Tibaa-Aat al-So-war al-raqa-may-ya
we have a machine for printing digital photos

ما هو الإسم من فضلك؟
maa hu-wa al-ism min faD-lak?
what's the name, please?

متى تريد استلام الصُّور؟
mata to-reed is-tilaam al-So-war?
when do you want them for?

يمكن تحميض الصُّور في خلال ساعة
yom-kin taH-meeD al-Soo-war fee khilaal saa-Aa
we can develop them in an hour

ستكون الصُّور جاهزة يوم الخميس ظهراً
sata-koon al-So-war jaa-hiza yawm al-kha-mees Zoh-ran
your photos will be ready on Thursday at noon

BANKS

Banks throughout the Arab world typically close at 3pm at the latest. In Egypt, for example, most banks are open between 8.30am and 2pm. Banks are usually open from Sunday to Thursday, although in some countries such as Lebanon you will find banks open on Fridays too.

ATM machines are widespread throughout the Arab world so you should have no problem withdrawing money on holiday. One thing to look into prior to travelling is the partnerships your local bank may have with banks in the country you are travelling to. This may not only save you some fees when you carry out a transaction such as changing money, but can also direct you to a safe cash machine to make your withdrawals from.

Money can be changed at markets, with a street vendor or at a local bank. Make sure beforehand that you are aware of the local exchange rate and that you discuss it with the trader before completing the transaction. You will usually be able to get a better rate in markets or with street vendors than at banks.

The basics

bank	بنك *bank*
bank account	حساب بنكى *Hi-saab ban-kee*
banknote	أوراق نقديّة *aw-raaq naq-day-ya*
cashpoint	ماكينة صرّاف آلي *makee-nat Sar-raaf aa-lee*
change	تغيير *tagh-yeer*
cheque	شيك *sheek*
coin	عملة معدنية *Aom-la maA-danay-ya*
commission	عمولة *Aomoo-la*
credit card	بطاقة ائتمان *beTaa-qat al-e'-ti-maan*
PIN (number)	الرقم الشخصى *al-raqam al-shakh-See*
transfer	تحويل *taH-weel*
Travellers Cheques®	شيكات سياحيّة *she-kaat se-yaa-Hay-ya*
withdrawal	سحب *saHb*
to change	يُغيِّر *yo-ghay-yir*
to transfer	يحوّل *yo-How-wil*

to withdraw   يسحب yas-Hab

Expressing yourself

where I can get some money changed?
أين أستطيع تغيير عمله؟
ayna as-ta-TeeA tagh-yeer Aom-la?

are banks open on Saturdays?
هل تعمل البنوك أيّام السبت؟
hal taA-mal al-bonook ay-yaam al-sabt?

I'm looking for a cashpoint
إنا أبحث عن ماكينة صرّاف آلي
ana ab-Hath Aan makee-nat Sar-raaf aa-lee

I'd like to change £100
أريد تغيير مائة جنيه إنجليزي
o-reed tagh-yeer ma-'at ji-neeh in-glee-zee

what commission do you charge?
عُمولتك كام؟
Aomol-tak kaam?

I'd like to transfer some money
أريد تخْويل بعض الأموال
o-reed taH-weel baAD al-am-waal

I'd like to report the loss of my credit card
أريد الإبلاغ عن فقد بطاقة إئتماني
o-reed al-ib-laagh Aan faqd be-Taa-qat al-e'-ti-maan

the cashpoint has swallowed my card
ابتلعت ماكينة الصراف الآلي بطاقتي
ib-talaAat makee-nat al-Sar-raaf al-aa-lee be-Taa-qatee

Understanding

من فضلك أدخِل البطاقة
please insert your card

من فضلك أدخِل رقمك الشخصي
please enter your PIN

من فضلك اختار المبلغ الذي تريد سحبه
please select amount for withdrawal

سحب مع إيصال
withdrawal with receipt

سحب دون إيصال
withdrawal without receipt

من فضلك اختر المبلغ الذي تريده
please select the amount you require

معطَّل – لا يعمل
out of service

POST OFFICES

Throughout the Arabic-speaking world it is relatively easy to send mail, particularly small letters and postcards. It takes between five and ten business days for mail to arrive in the United Kingdom. In Egypt and most other countries, post offices are typically open between 8.30am and 3pm daily, except Fridays. Some post offices in Cairo stay open 24 hours a day. Mail boxes can be found on most street corners but you should pay attention to what colour they are. In Egypt, red mail boxes are for mail being delivered within Egypt, blue mail boxes for overseas mail and green boxes for Cairo mail. Sending larger packages is sometimes difficult because of Customs procedures, so take an Arabic-speaking friend to the post office with you if possible. In most major cities you will also find international mail carriers, which may be an alternative to the national post offices. However, these companies tend to be significantly more expensive and don't necessarily provide a quicker delivery service.

The basics

airmail	بريد جوى	ba-reed jow-wee
envelope	مظروف	maZ-roof
letter	خطاب	khe-Taab
mail	بريد	ba-reed
parcel	طر د	Tard
post	بريد	ba-reed
postbox	صندوق بريد	Son-dooq ba-reed
postcard	بطاقه بريدية	beTaa-qa ba-ree-day-ya
postcode	رمز بريدى	ramz ba-ree-dee
post office	مكتب بريد	mak-tab ba-reed
stamp	طابع بريد	Taa-biA ba-reed
to post	يرسل بالبريد	yor-sil bel-ba-reed
to send	يرسل	yor-sil
to write	يكتب	yak-tob

Expressing yourself

is there a post office around here?
هل يوجد مكتب بريد بالقرب من هنا؟
hal yoo-jad mak-tab ba-reed bil-qorb min hu-na?

is there a postbox near here?
هل يوجد صندوق بريد بالقرب من هنا؟
hal yoo-jad Son-dooq ba-reed bil-qorb min hu-na?

is the post office open on Saturdays?
هل يعمل مكتب البريد أيام السبت؟
hal yaA-mal mak-tab al-ba-reed ay-yaam al-sabt?

what time does the post office close?
متى يغلق مكتب البريد؟
mata yogh-liq mak-tab al-ba-reed?

do you sell stamps?
هل تباع طوابع بريد هنا؟
hal tobaaA Tawaa-biA ba-reed hu-na?

I'd like … stamps for the UK, please
أريد طوابع بريد لبريطانيا من فضلك
o-reed Tawaa-biA ba-reed le bree-Tan-ya min faD-lak

how long will it take to arrive?
كم يستغرق الوقت حتى نصل؟
kam yas-tagh-riq al-waqt Hat-ta ta Sil?

where can I buy envelopes?
أين يمكن شراء مظاريف؟
ayna yom-kin she-ra' maZa-reef?

is there any post for me?
هل يوجد خطابات لي؟
hal yoo-jad kheTa-baat lee?

Understanding

أخرموعد لتجميع البريد	last collection
احمل بعناية	handle with care
الراسل	sender

قابل للكسر
أول تجميع للبريد

fragile
first collection

سيصل في مابين ثلاثة وخمسة ايام
sa-ya-Sil fee-ma bay-na tha-la-tha wa kham-sat ay-yaam
it'll take between three and five days

INTERNET CAFÉS AND E-MAIL

Throughout the Arabic-speaking world Internet access is quite readily available, especially in the major urban centres. Most Internet cafés and other places with Internet access will be recognizable by a sign reading INTERNET or @.

Prior to using the internet, you should always check the price per half hour or hour, even if there is a posted rate. Also, try and keep track of how much time you spend on the Internet so that you are not overcharged. Some Internet cafés will allow you to connect using your own laptop.

Most of the keyboards used throughout the Gulf region are standard English keyboards with the QWERTY layout.

The basics

at sign	مفتاح علامة	mof-taH Aala-mat
e-mail address	عنوان البريد الإلكتروني	Aon-waan al-ba-reed al-elek-tro-nee
Internet café	مقهى إنترنت	maq-ha internet
key	مفتاح	mof-taH
keyboard	لوحة المفاتيح	low-Hat al-mafaa-teeH
to copy	ينسخ	yan-sakh
to cut	يقص	ya-qoS
to delete	يحذف	yaH-dhif
to download	ينزّل	yo-naz-zil
to e-mail somebody	... يرسل إيميل إلي	yor-sil email ila ...
to paste	يضيف	yo-Deef
to receive	يتلقّي	yata-laq-qa
to save	يحفظ	yaH-faZ
to send an e-mail	يرسل إيميل	yor-sil email

Expressing yourself

is there an Internet café near here?

هل يوجد مقهى إنترنت قريب من هنا؟

hal yoo-jad maq-ha internet qa-reeb min hu-na?

do you have an e-mail address?

هل لديك عنوان بريد إلكتروني؟

hal laday-ka Aon-waan ba-reed elek-tro-nee?

how do I get online?

كيف يُمكن الدخول على الإنترنت؟

keyfa yom-kin al-do-khool Ala al-internet?

I'd just like to check my e-mails

أريد فقط مراجعة بريدي الإلكتروني

o-reed faqaT moraa-jaAat ba-reed-ee al-elek-tro-nee

would you mind helping me? I'm not sure what to do

هل تستطيع مساعدتي؟ ليس لديّ خبرة كافية؟

hal tas-ta-TeeA mo-saa-Aadatee? lay-sa laday-ya khib-ra kaa-feya?

I can't find the at sign on this keyboard

لا أعرف أين علامة @ على لوحة المفاتيح

laa aA-rif ayna Aalaa-mat Aala low-Hat al-mafaa-teeH

it's not working

هذا لا يعمل

ha-dha laa yaA-mal

there's something wrong with the computer, it's frozen

يوجد مشكلة بالحاسوب. إنه لا يستجيب للأوامر

yoo-jad mosh-kila bil-Haa-soob. in-naho laa yasta-jeeb lil-awaa-mir

how much will it be for half an hour?

كم يكلف الإستخدام لمدة نصف ساعة؟

kam youkal-lif al-istikh-dam li-mod-dat neSf saa-Aa?

when do I pay?

متى يجب الدفع؟

mata ya-jib al-dafA?

Understanding

البريد الوارد	inbox
البريد الصادر	outbox

يجب عليك الإنتظارحوالي عشرين دقيقة
ya-jib Aalay-ka al-in-ti Zaar Hawaa-lee Ash-reen da-qee-qa
you'll have to wait for 20 minutes or so

يمكنك طلب مساعدة إذا لم تكن تعرف طريقة التشغيل
yom-kinak Talab mosaa-Aada idha lam takon taA-rif Ta-reeq-at al-tash-gheel
just ask if you're not sure what to do

فقط أدخل كلمة السر هذه للتسجيل
faqaT ad-khil kalimat al-sirr ha-dhe-he lil-tas-jeel
just enter this password to log on

TELEPHONE

Most public telephones do not have their own phone numbers, and therefore can only be used for outgoing calls. All phones take either pre-paid cards or coins. Phone cards can be purchased in most general stores or souvenir shops, or from street vendors.

Using your own mobile phone, however, will be more convenient. In some countries, such as Syria, you can get a SIM card free as long as you purchase a few pounds' worth of credit at the same time. Numbers are activated immediately and you can use the phone to make local or international calls. In other countries, such as Lebanon, a SIM card is more expensive, but you may decide it is worth it for the convenience of being able to make calls whenever you like and not have to rely on finding a public telephone in unfamiliar surroundings.

Some places offer international calls at reduced rates, which is often cheaper then using a pre-paid phonecard to call home. When calling the UK, dial 00 44 then the local number (drop the 0 from the area code). To call the US, dial 00 1, then the area code and phone number.

The basics

answering machine	جهاز الرَّد على المكالمات *ji-haaz al-radd Ala al-mokaa-lamaat*
call	مُكالمة *mokaa-lama*
directory enquiries	دليل التليفونات *da-leel al-tele-foo-naat*
hello	أهلاً *ah-lan*
international call	مكالمة دوليّة *mokaa-lama dow-lay-ya*
local call	مكالمة محليّة *mokaa-lama maHal-lay-ya*
message	رسالة *ri-saa-la*
mobile	محمول *maH-mool*
national call	مكالمة داخلية *mokaa-lama daa-khe-lay-ya*
phone	تليفون *tele-foon*
phone book	دليل التليفون *da-leel al-tele-foon*
phone box	كشك تليفون *koshk tele-foon*

phonecard	بطاقة إتّصال هاتفي	be-Ta-qat et-ti-Saal haa-te-fee
phone call	مكالمة تليفونيّة	mokaa-lama tele-foo-nay-ya
phone number	رقم تليفون	raqam tele-foon
ringtone	نغمة	naghama
telephone	تليفون	tele-foon
top-up card	كارت شحن	kart shaHn
Yellow Pages ®	دليل الخدمات المهنية	da-leel al-khed-maat al-meha-nay-ya
to call somebody	يتلفنّ	yat-taSil

Expressing yourself

where can I buy a phonecard?
أين يمكن شراء بطاقة إتّصال هاتفي؟
ayna yom-kin she-ra' be-Ta-qat et-ti-Saal haa-te-fee?

a ...-pound top-up card, please
بطاقة شحن للمحمول ب ... جنيه من فضلك
be-Ta-qat shaHn lil-maH-mool bi ...ji-neeh min faD-lak

I'd like to make a reverse-charge call
أريد إجراء مكالمة يدفع ثمنها المستقبِل
o-reed ij-raa' mokaa-lama yad-faA thama-naha al-mos-taq-bil

is there a phone box near here, please?
هل يوجد كشك تليفون قريب من هنا من فضلك؟
hal yoo-jad koshk tele-foon qa-reeb min hu-na min faD-lak?

can I plug my phone in here to recharge it?
ممكن أوصّل شاحن تليفوني بالكهرباء هنا؟
mom-kin o-waS-Sil shaa-Hin tele-foo-nee bil-kah-raba hu-na?

do you have a mobile number?
هل لديك رقم محمول؟
hal laday-ka raqam maH-mool?

where can I contact you?
أين أستطيع الإتصال بك؟
ayna asta-TeeA al-et-ti-Saal beek?

did you get my message?
هل وصلتك رسالتي؟
hal waSa-latka re-saa-latee?

Understanding

الرقم الذى طلبته لم يتم التعرف عليه
al-raqam al-la-dhee Talab-tah lam ya-timm al-ta-Aar-rof Aa-layh
the number you have dialled has not been recognized

من فضلك، إضغط على زر الإعادة
min faD-lak. iD-ghaT Ala zerr al-eAa-da
please press the hash key

MAKING A CALL

Expressing yourself

hello, this is David Brown (speaking)
أهلاً! أنا دافيد براون
ah-lan! ana david brown

hello, could I speak to ..., please?
أهلاً! هل ممكن أن أتحدث إلى ... من فضلك؟
ah-lan! hal mom-kin an ila ... min faD-lak?

hello, is that Mohammad?
أهلاً! هل أنت محمد؟
ah-lan! hal an-ta mo-Ham-mad?

do you speak English?
هل تتحدث إنجليزي؟
hal tata-Had-dath in-glee-zee?

could you speak more slowly, please?
تحدّث ببطئ أكثر لو سمحت؟
ta-Had-dath be-boT' ak-thar, low sa-maHt?

I can't hear you, could you speak up, please?
لأستطيع سماعك.هل ممكن أن ترفع صوتك من فضلك؟
laa as-ta-TeeA sa-maa-Aak. hal mom-kin an tar-faA Sow-tak min faD-lak?

could you tell him/her I called?
هل ممكن أن تخبره / تخبرها أننى اتّصلتُ؟
hal mom-kin an tokh-bir-ho/takh-bir-ha an-na-nee et-ta-Salt?

could you ask him/her to call me back?

هل ممكن أن تطلب منه / منها الإتّصال بي لاحقاً؟

hal mom-kin an taT-lob min-ho/min-ha al-et-ti-Sal bee laa-Hiqan

I'll call back later

سأتّصل لاحقاً

sa-at-taSil laa-Hiqan

my name is ... and my number is ...

إسمى ... ورقمى هو ...

is-mee ... wa raqamee hu-wa ...

do you know when he/she might be available?

ما هو الوقت المناسب للإتّصال به / بها؟

maa hu-wa al-waqt al-monaa-sib lil-et-ti-Saal be-hee/be-ha?

thank you, goodbye

شكراً! مع السلامة

shok-ran. mAa al-salaa-ma!

Understanding

من المتحدّث؟

man al-mota-Had-dith?

who's calling?

لقد اتّصلت بالرقم الخطأ

laqad et-ta-Salta bel-raqam al-kha-TA'

you've got the wrong number

هو/ هى ليس/ ليست هنا الان

hu-wa/he-ya lay-sa/lay-sat hu-na al-'aan

he's/she's not here at the moment

هل تُريد ترك رسالة؟

hal to-reed tark ri-saa-la?

do you want to leave a message?

سوف أخبِرُه/ أخبِرُها أنّك اتّصلت

sow-fa okh-bir-ho/okh-bir-ha an-naka et-ta-Salt

I'll tell him/her you called

سوف أطلب منه/ منها الإتصال بك لاحقاً
sow-fa aT-lob min-hu/min-ha al-et-ti-Saal bika laa-Hiqan
I'll ask him/her to call you back

انتظر!
in-taZir!
hold on!

سوف أعطبه / أعطيها لك
sow-fa oA-Tee-he/oA-Tee-ha lak
I'll just hand you over to him/her

PROBLEMS

Expressing yourself

I don't know the code
لا أعرفُ مفتاح المدينة
laa aA-rif mof-taH al-madee-na

it's engaged
الخط مشغول
al-khaTT mash-ghool

there's no reply
ليس هناك رد
lay-sa hu-naa-k radd

I couldn't get through
لم أستطيع الإتّصال
lam as-ta-TeeA al-et-ti-Saal

I don't have much credit left on my phone
ليس لدي رصيد كافي
lay-sa laday-ya ra-Seed kaa-fee

we're about to get cut off
الخط على وشك الإنقطاع
al-khaTT Alaa wa-shak al-en-qey-TaaA

the reception's really bad

الإستقبال سيّئ للغاية

al-is-tiq-baal say-ye' lil-ghaay-ya

I can't get a signal

لا أستطيع التقاط الشبكة

laa as-ta-TeeA ilti-qaaT al-sha-ba-ka

Understanding

أنا أسمعك بصعوبة

ana as-maAak be-Sa-Aoo-ba
I can hardly hear you

الخط سيّئ

al-khaTT say-ye'
it's a bad line

Common abbreviations

Aa-mal ت. عمل = work (number)

man-zel ت. منزل = home (number)

maH-mool ت. محمول = mobile (number)

HEALTH

Prior to your departure you should check with your doctor to see if you need any vaccinations. Travelling throughout North Africa and the Middle East is generally safe; however some areas are considered to have a slight risk of malaria or yellow fever so ensure that you take all necessary precautions.

Medical facilities for non-emergency matters are adequate in most major cities. Once you travel out of the tourist areas or into less populated areas you will find that your access to medical facilities becomes somewhat limited so try to take some basic medication with you, such as painkillers.

Contacting a doctor in Egypt is easy. If you do not know someone in the country who can refer you to one with a private practice, then you can go to a hospital and be treated there. Alternatively, if you find a doctor's office on the street you can walk in and ask for an appointment. Your holiday insurance policy should cover most visits and minor procedures, but it's worth checking which doctors and hospitals will accept your insurance.

Medicine can be bought from pharmacies, which are usually open late into the evening most days of the week. If you are feeling ill, but not ill enough to go and see a doctor, a pharmacist may be able to suggest an over-the-counter remedy.

The basics

allergy	حساسية	Hasa-say-ya
ambulance	إسعاف	is-Aaaf
aspirin	اسبرين	as-be-reen
blood	دم	damm
broken	مكسور	mak-soor
casualty (department)	قسم الطوارئ	qism al-Ta-waa-re'
chemist's	صيدلية	Say-da-lay-ya
condom	عازل طبي	Aa-zil Tib-be
dentist	طبيب الأسنان	Tabeeb as-naan

diarrhoea	إسهال is-haal
doctor	طبيب Tabeeb
food poisoning	تسمم غذائى ta-sam-mom ghi-zaa-'ee
GP	مارس عام momaa-ris Aaam
gynaecologist	طبيب أمراض نساء Tabeeb am-raaD ni-sa'
hospital	مستشفى mos-tashfa
infection	عدوى Aad-wa
medicine	دواء dawaa'
painkiller	مسكن للألم mo-sak-kin lil-alam
periods	دورة شهرية dow-ra shah-ray-ya
plaster	لاصق طبى laa-Siq Tib-be
rash	طفح جلدى TafH jel-dee
spot	بقعة boq-Aa
sunburn	لفحة شمس laf-Hit shams
tablet	أقراص aq-raaS
temperature	حرارة Ha-raa-ra
vaccination	تطعيم taT-Aeem
X-ray	أشعة إكس ashiA-Aat x
to disinfect	يطهر yo-Tah-hir
to faint	يشعر بإغماء yash-Aor be-egh-maa'
to vomit	يتقيأ yata-qay-ya'

Expressing yourself

does anyone have an aspirin/a tampon/a plaster, by any chance?

هل يوجد أحد لديه أسبرين / فوطه صحية نسائية/ لاصق طبى؟

hal yoo-jad aHad laday-he as-be-reen/foo-Ta SiH-Hay-ya ni-saa-'eya/laa-Siq Tib-be?

I need to see a doctor

أريد رؤية طبيب

o-reed ro'-yat Tabeeb

where can I find a doctor?

أين أستطيع إيجاد طبيب؟

ayna as-ta-TeeA ee-jaad Tabeeb?

I'd like to make an appointment for today

أريد تحديد موعد اليوم

o-reed taH-deed mow-Aed al-yawm

as soon as possible

بأسرع مايمكن
be-as-raA ma yom-kin

no, it doesn't matter

لا. ليس مهما
laa. lay-sa mohim-man

can you send an ambulance to ...

يمكن إرسال سيارة إسعاف إلى ...
mom-kin er-saal say-ya-rat es-Aaaf ila ...

I've broken my glasses

إنكسرت نظارتى
in-kasarat naZ-Zaa-ratee

I've lost a contact lens

فقدت عدسة لاصقة
faqad-to Aadasa laa-Siqa

Understanding

عيادة طبيب
Aeya-dat Tabeeb
doctor's surgery

(تذكرة طبية) روشتة
ro-shit-ta (tadh-kara Tib-bay-ya)
prescription

قسم الطوارئ
qism al-Ta-waa-re'
casualty department

لا يوجد موعد متاح حتى يوم الخميس
laa yoo-jad mow-Aed motaaH Hat-ta yawm al-khamees
there are no available appointments until Thursday

هل يوم الجمعة الساعة الثانية ظهرا مناسب؟
hal yawm al-jomAa al-saa-Aa al-tha-ne-ya Zoh-ran monaa-sib?
is Friday at 2pm OK?

AT THE DOCTOR'S OR THE HOSPITAL

Expressing yourself

I have an appointment with Dr ...

لدى موعد مع دكتور ...
laday-ya mow-Aed mAa dok-toor ...

I don't feel very well

أشعر بأني لست على مايرام
ash-Aor be-an-ne las-to Ala mayoraam

I feel very weak

اشعر بضعف شديد
ash-Aor be-DaAf sha-deed

I don't know what it is

لأعرف ماهو بالضبط
laa aA-rif maa hu-wa bil-DabT

I've been bitten/stung by ...

لدغتني - قرصتني ...
ladaghat-nee/qaraSat-nee ...

I've got a headache

أشعر بصداع
ash-Aor be-SodaaA

I've got toothache/stomachache

أشعر بصداع / بألم في الأسنان
ash-Aor be-SodaaA/be-alam fee al-as-naan

I've got a sore throat

أشعر بألم في الحلق
ash-Aor be-alam fee al-Halq

my back hurts

ظهري يؤلمني
Zah-ree yo'-lim-nee

it hurts

هذا يؤلم
ha-dha yo'-lim

it hurts here
الألم هنا
al-alam hu-na

I feel sick
أشعر بالغثيان
ash-Aor bel-ghatha-yaan

it's got worse
الحالة تزداد سوء
al-Haa-la tadh-daad soo'

it's been three days
منذ حوالي ثلاث أيام
mon-dho Ha-waa-lee tha-laath ay-yaam

it started last night
بدأ منذ الليلة الماضية
bada'a mon-dho al-lay-la al-maa-De-ya

it's never happened to me before
لم يحدث لي هذا مطلقا
lam yaH-doth lee ha-dha moT-laqan

I've got a temperature
لدي ارتفاع في درجة الحرارة
laday-ya ir-ti-faaA fee da-ra-jat al-Har-ar-a

I have asthma
أعاني من الربو (أزمة)
oAaa-nee min al-raboo (az-ma)

I have a heart condition
أنا مريض بالقلب
ana ma-reeD bel-qalb

I've been on antibiotics for a week and I'm not getting any better
أخذت مضاد حيوي لمدة أسبوع ولا أشعر بتحسن
a-khdh-to mo-DaaD Hayawee li-mod-dat os-booA wa laa ash-Aor beta-Has-son

it itches
أشعر بالحكَّة في هذا المكان
ash-Aor bel-Hak-ka fee ha-dha al-makaan

HEALTH

I'm on the pill/the minipill
أنا أتناول حبوب منع الحمل
ana atanaa-wal Ho-boob manA al-Haml

I'm ... months pregnant
أنا حامل في الشهر ...
ana Haa-mil fee al-shahr ...

I'm allergic to penicillin
عندي حساسية ضد البنسلين
Aen-dee Hasa-say-ya DiD al-ben-se-leen

I've twisted my ankle
الجزء مفصل قدمي
in-jazaA mif-Sal qada-mee

I fell and hurt my back
سقطت وأصيب ظهري
saqaT-To wa oo-See-ba Zah-ree

I've had a blackout
فقدت الوعى لفترة
faqad-to al-waAy le-fatrah

I've lost a filling
سقط الحشو من احدى أسناني
saqaTa al-Hasho min iH-da as-naa-nee

is it serious?
هل هو خطير ؟
hal hu-wa kha-Teer?

is it contagious?
هل هو معدى؟
hal hu-wa moA-dee?

how is he/she?
كيف حاله/ حالها؟
keyfa Haa-loh/Haa-laha?

how much do I owe you?
كم يجب علي أن أدفع؟
kam ya-jib Alay-ya an adfA?

can I have a receipt so I can get the money refunded?

ممكن آخذ إيصال حتى استرد المبلغ؟

mom-kin aa-khodh ee-Saal Hat-ta asta-rid al-mab-lagh?

Understanding

تفضل بالجلوس فى حجرة الإنتظار
ta-faD-Dal bel-jo-loos fee Hoj-rat al-en-tiZaar
if you'd like to take a seat in the waiting room

أى مكان يؤلمك؟
ay makaan yo'-limak/yo'-limik?
where does it hurt?

خذ نفس عميق
khoz nafas Aa-meeq
take a deep breath

استلقى على ظهرك من فضلك
is-tal-qee Ala Zah-rak/Zah-rik, min faD-lak
lie down, please

هل تشعر بالألم حين أضغط هنا؟
hal tash-Aor/tash-Ao-reen bel-alam Hee-na aD-ghaT hu-na?
does it hurt when I press here?

هل تم تطعيمك ضد...؟
hal tam-ma taT-Aee-mak Did…?
have you been vaccinated against …?

هل لديك حساسية ضد...؟
hal laday-ka/laday-ke Hasa-say-ya Did…?
are you allergic to …?

هل تأخذ أدوية أخرى؟
hal ta'-khodh ad-we-ya okh-ra?
are you taking any other medication?

سأكتب لك روشتته (تذكرة طبية)
sa-'ak-tob laka ro-shit-ta (tadh-kara Tib-be-ya)
I'm going to write you a prescription

سيزول الألم خلال أيام
sa-yazool al-alam khi-laal ay-yaam
it should clear up in a few days

سيندمل الجرح بسرعة
sa-yan-damil al-jarH be-sor-Aa
it should heal quickly

ستحتاج عملية جراحية
sa-taH-taaj Aama-lay-ya jiraa-Hay-ya
you're going to need an operation

تفضل بالعودة لتراني بعد أسبوع
ta-faD-Dal bil-Aow-da le-taraa-nee bAda os-booA
come back and see me in a week

AT THE CHEMIST'S

Expressing yourself

I'd like a box of plasters, please
أريد علبة لاصق طبى من فضلك!
o-reed Aol-bat laa-Siq Tib-be min faD-lak!

could I have something for a bad cold?
أريد علاج لنزلة برد شديدة!
o-reed Aelaaj le-naz-lat bard sha-dee-da!

I need something for a cough
أريد علاجاً للكحة!
o-reed Aelaaj lil-koH-Ha

I'm allergic to aspirin
عندي حساسية ضد الأسبرين
Aan-de Hasa-say-ya Did al-as-be-reen

I'd like to try a homeopathic remedy
أريد تجربة العلاج بالمثل (الهوميوبثى)
o-reed taj-ribat al-Aelaaj bel-mithl (homeopathy)

I'd like a bottle of solution for soft contact lenses

اريد زجاجة محلول طبي لعدساتي اللا صقة

o-reed zojaa-jat maH-lool Tib-be le-Adasaa-tee al-laa-Siqa

Understanding

يضع	apply
يصرف على الروشتة فقط	available on prescription only
كبسولات	capsule
مخاطر الدواء	contra-indications
كريم	cream
مرهم	ointment
أعراض جانبية محتملة	possible side effects
بودرة	powder
لبوس (أقماع)	suppositories
شراب	syrup
أقراص	tablet
يؤخذ ثلاث مرات قبل الأكل يوميا	take three times a day before meals

PROBLEMS AND EMERGENCIES

Beware of pickpockets, especially in tourist areas. If you lose something in a market or are being bothered by someone, you should look for the very identifiable "tourist police". You will find them in most major tourist areas and they are recognizable by their uniforms which have an armband with the insignia "tourist police" or "police" written on the back in Arabic and English. Although the word *bo-lees* is widely used for police, the formal word is *shor-Ta*. Either word will be understood.

The basics

accident	حادث	*Haa-dith*
ambulance	إسعاف	*is-Aaf*
broken	مكسور	*mak-soor*
disabled	معاق	*moo-Aaq*
doctor	طبيب	*Tabeeb*
emergency	طوارئ	*Ta-waa-re'*
fire brigade	مطافى	*maTaa-fee*
fire	حريق	*Ha-reeq*
hospital	مستشفى	*mos-tashfa*
ill	مريض	*ma-reeD*
injured	مصاب	*moo-Sab*
late	متأخر	*mota-'akh-khir*
police	شرطة	*shor-Ta*

Expressing yourself

can you help me?

ممكن ان تساعدني من فضلك؟

mom-kin an tosaa-Aednee min faD-lak?

help!
النجدة!
al-naj-da!

fire!
حريق!
Ha-reeq!

be careful!
إحذر!
iH-dhar!

it's an emergency!
نها حالة طوارئ!
in-naha Haa-lat Ta-waa-re'!

could I borrow your phone, please?
مكن أستعير تليفونك لوسمحت؟
mom-kin as-ta-Aeer tele-foo-nak, low sa-maHt?

there's been an accident
كان هناك حادث
ka-na hu-nak Haa-dith

does anyone here speak English?
هل يوجد احد هنا يتحدث إجليزي؟
hal yoo-jad aHad hu-na yata-Had-dath in-glee-zee?

I need to contact the British consulate
أريد أن أتصل بالقنصلية البريطانية
o-reed an at-ta-Sil bil-qonSo-lay-ya al-bree-Ta-ney-ya

where's the nearest police station?
أين أقرب قسم شرطة هنا؟
ayna aq-rab qism shor-Ta hu-na?

what do I have to do?
ماذا يجب أن أفعل؟
ma-dha ya-jib an af-Aal?

my passport/credit card has been stolen
سُرق جواز سفرى ــ بطاقة إئتماني
soriqa jawaaz safaree/be-Ta-qat al-i-ti-ma-nee

my bag's been snatched

خُطفت حقيبة يدي

khoTifat Ha-qee-bat ya-dee

I've lost …

فَقدتُ …

faqad-to …

I've been attacked

تَعرضتُ لإعتداء

ta-Aar-raD-to li-eA-ti-da'

my son/daughter is missing

تاه ابني تاهت إبنتي

ta-ha ib-nee/ta-hat ib-na-tee

my car's been towed away

سحب الونش سيارتي

sa-Haba al-wensh say-ya-ra-tee

I've broken down

تعطّلت سيّارتي

taAaT-Talat say-ya-ra-tee

my car's been broken into

تم كسر سيّارتي وسرقتها

tam-ma kasr say-ya-ra-tee wa sareqat-ha

there's a man following me

هناك رجل يتبعني

hu-naka rajol yat-baA-nee

is there disabled access?

هل هناك مدخل للمعاقين؟

hal hu-naka mad-khal lil-moAaa-qeen?

can you keep an eye on my things for a minute?

هلا يمكنك ملاحظة أمتعتي للحظة؟

hal yom-kinak molaa-HaZat am-teAa-tee li-laH-Za?

he's drowning, get help!

إنه يغرق. اطلب النجدة!

in-naho yagh-raq. oT-lob al-naj-da!

Understanding

احذر الكلاب!
ih-dhar al-kilaab!
beware of the dog

احذرالألغام
ih-dhar al-al-ghaam
beware of mines

خدمة طوارىء السيّارات المعطلة
khid-mat Ta-waa-re' al-say-ya-raat al-moAat-Tala
breakdown service

مخرج الطوارئ
makh-raj al-Ta-waa-re'
emergency exit

أمتعة مفقودة
am-ti Aa maf-qooda
lost property

شرطة الإنقاذ النهري
shor-Tat al-inqaadh al-nah-ree
river rescue police

معطَّل
moAat-Tal
out of order

خدمات شرطة الطوارىء
khid-mat shor-Tat al-Ta-waa-re'
police emergency services

POLICE

Expressing yourself

I want to report something stolen
أريد أن أبلّغ عن شيئٍ مفقود
o-reed an o-bal-legh An shay' maf-qood

I need a document from the police for my insurance company

أريد مستند رسمي من الشرطة لشركة التأمين

o-reed mos-tanad ras-me min al-shor-Ta li-sharikat al-ta'-meen

Understanding

Filling in forms

إسم العائلة	surname
الإسم الأول	first name
عنوان	address
الرمز البريدي	postcode
البلد	country
الجنسية	nationality
تاريخ الميلاد	date of birth
محل الميلاد	place of birth
السن	age
مدة الإقامة	duration of stay
تاريخ الوصول - المغادرة	arrival/departure date
المهنة	occupation
رقم جواز السفر	passport number

هناك جمارك على هذا

hu-naka jamaa-rik Ala ha-dha

there's Customs duty to pay on this item

افتح هذه الشنطة من فضلك

if-taH ha-dhe-he al-shan-Ta min faD-lak

would you open this bag, please?

ماذا فقدتَ؟

ma-dha faqadta?

what's missing?

متى حدث هذا؟

mata Hadatha ha-dha?

when did this happen?

أين تقيم؟

ayna to-qeem?

where are you staying?

مكن توصفه - توصفها؟
mom-kin tow-Sif-ho/tow-Sif-ha?
can you describe him/her/it?

املأ هذا النموذج من فضلك
em-la' ha-dha al-na-mo-dhaj min faD-lak
would you fill in this form, please?

قم بالتوقيع هنا من فضلك؟
qom be al-tow-qeeA hu-na min faD-lak
would you sign here, please?

Some informal epressions

قبضت الشرطة عليَّ *qabaDat al-shor-Ta Aa-lay-ya* I've been arrested
عسكري مرور *As-ka-ree mo-roor* traffic warden
عسكري *As-ka-ree* policeman
ضابط شرطة *Da-biT shor-Ta* police officer
حرامي *Ha-raa-mee* thief
نشّال *nash-shaal* pickpocket

TIME AND DATE

The Islamic lunar calendar is important, as it shows the dates of the Islamic religious feasts throughout the year. However, although the majority of Egyptian inhabitants are Muslims, they tend to follow the Gregorian calendar when expressing dates.

TIME

The basics

after	بعد baAd
already	بالفعل bil-fiAl
always	دائماً daa-'eman
at lunchtime	في وقت الغذاء fee waqt al-ghadha'
at the beginning/end of	في بداية / نهاية fee be-daa-yat/ne-haa-yat
at the moment	الآن al-'aan
before	قبل qabl
between ... and ...	ما بين ... و ... ma bayn ...wa ...
day	يوم yawm
during	أثناء ath-na'
early	مبكّراً mobak-kiran
evening	مساءً masaa-an
for a long time	لمدة طويلة le-mod-da Ta-wee-la
from ... to ...	من ... إلي ... min ... ila ...
from time to time	بين الحين والأخري bayn al-Heen wa al-okh-raa
in a little while	لوقت قصير le waqt qa-Seer
in the evening	في المساء fee al-masaa'
in the middle of	خلال khi-laal
last	ماضي maa-Dee
late	متأخر mota-'kh-khir
midday	وقت الظّهيرة waqt al-Za-hee-ra
midnight	منتصف اللّيل mon-taSaf al-layl
month	شهر shahr
morning	صباح Sa-baH

never	مطلقاً moT-laqan
net	قادم qaa-dim
night	ليل layl
not yet	ليس بعد lay-sa baAd
now	الحين al-Heen
occasionally	في بعض الأوقات fee baAD al-aw-qaat
often	غالباً ghaa-liban
rarely	نادراً naa-diran
recently	مؤخّراً mo'akh-kharan
since	منذُ mondh
sometimes	أحياناً aH-yan-an
soon	قريباً qaree-ban
still	ما زال ma-zaal
straightaway	حالاً Haa-lan
until	حتّي Hat-ta
week	أسبوع os-booA
weekend	نهاية الأسبوع ne-haa-yat al-os-booA
year	عام Aam

TIME AND DATE

Expressing yourself

see you soon!
أراك قريباً
araa-ka qaree-ban

see you later!
أراك فيما بعد
araa-ka fee-ma baAd

see you on Monday!
يوم الإثنين أراك
araa-ka yawm al-eth-nayn

have a good weekend!
أتمنّي لك وقت ممتع في عطلة نهاية الأسبوع
ataman-na laka waqt mom-tiA fee AoT-lat ne-haa-yat al-os-booA

sorry I'm late
آسف علي التأخير / آسفة
aa-sif / aa-sifa Ala al-ta'-kheer

135

I haven't been there yet

لم أصِل إلى المكان بعد

lam a-Sil ila al-makaan baAd

I haven't had time to …

لم يكن لدي وقت ل ...

lam yakon laday-ya waqt le …

I've got plenty of time

لديّ متّسع من الوقت

laday-ya mot-tasaA min al-waqt

I'm in a rush

أنا مستعجل

ana mis-taA-jil

hurry up!

أسْرِع!

as-riA!

just a minute, please

انتظر دقيقة من فضلك

in-taZir da-qee-qa min faD-lak

I had a late night

نِمتُ مُتأخِّراً

nimto mota'kh-khiran

I got up very early

استيْقَظتُ مبكِّراً جداً

is-tay-qaZ-to mobak-kiran jid-dan

I waited ages

انْتَظرتُ طويلاً

in-taZar-to Ta-wee-lan

I have to get up very early tomorrow to catch my plane

يجب أن أستيقظ مبكراً غداً لأَلْحَق موعد الطّائرة

ya-jib an as-tay-qiZ mobak-kiran ghadan le-al-Haq mow-Aed al-Taa-'e-rah

we only have four days left

لم يتبقّ لدينا هنا سوى أربعة أيّام

lam yata-baq-qa laday-na hu-na so-wa ar-baAat ay-yaam

TIME AND DATE

THE DATE

The basics

... ago	منذُ ... *mondh ...*
at the beginning/end of ...	في بداية / نهاية ... *fee be-daa-yat/ne-haa-yat ...*
in the middle of ...	خلال ... *khi-laal ...*
in two days' time	في غضون يومين *fee gho-Doon yaw-mayn*
last night	ليلة أمس *lay-lat ams*
the day after tomorrow	بعد غد *baAd ghad*
the day before yesterday	أمس الأول *ams al-aw-wal*
today	اليوم *al-yawm*
tomorrow	غداً *ghadan*
tomorrow morning/ afternoon/evening	صباح الغدْ / بعد ظهر الغدْ / مساء الغدْ *Sa-baaH al-ghad/baAd Zohr al-ghad/masaa' al-ghad*
yesterday	أمس *ams*
yesterday morning/ afternoon/evening	صباح أمسْ / بعد ظهر أمسْ / مساء أمسْ *sa-baaH ams/baAd Zohr ams/masaa' ams*

Expressing yourself

I was born in 1975

وُلدتُ عام 1975

wolit-to Aam alf wa tisAo-me-'a wa khamsa wa sab-Aeen

I came here a few years ago

جئتُ إلى هنا منذ بضع سنين

je'-to ila hu-na mondho biDA see-neen

I spent a month here last summer

قضيت شهراً هنا الصيف الماضي

qa-Day-to shah-ran hu-na al-Sayf al-maa-Dee

I was here last year at the same time

جئت إلى هنا في نفس الوقت من العام الماضي

je'-to ila hu-na fee nafs al-waqt min al-Aam al-maa-Dee

what's the date today?
ما هو تاريخ اليوم؟
ma hu-wa taa-reekh al-yawm?

what day is it today?
في أي يوم نحن ؟
fee ayy yawm naH-noo?

it's the 1st of May
إنه الأوّل من مايو
in-naho al-aw-wal min maa-yoo

I'm staying until Sunday
سأبقى هنا حتى يوم الأحد
sa-ab-qa hu-na Hat-ta yawm al-aHad

we're leaving tomorrow
سنُغادر غداً
sa-noghaa-dir ghadan

I already have plans for Tuesday
أنا مشغول يوم الثلاثاء
ana mash-ghool yawm al-thola-thaa'

Understanding

مرة / مرتان
mar-ra/mar-ra-tan
once/twice

ثلاث مرّات في السّاعة / اليوم
tha-lath mar-rat fee al-saa-Aa/al-yawm
three times an hour/a day

كل يوم
koll yawm
every day

كل يوم أحد
koll yawm aHad
every Sunday

تم بناؤه في مُنْتَصف القرن التاسع عشر
tam-ma be-naa-oh fee mon-taSaf al-qarn al-taa-siA Ashar
it was built in the mid-nineteenth century

يكون المكان هنا مُزدَحِم بالصيف
ya-koon al-makaan hu-na moz-daHim bil Sayf
it gets very busy here in the summer

متى سـتُغادِر؟
mata sa-toghaa-dir?
when are you leaving?

إلى متى ستظلَّ هنا؟
ila mata sata-Zall/sata-Zal-leen hu-na?
how long are you staying?

THE TIME

(i)

If someone asks you what time it is (*al-saa-Aa kaam?*) you can respond simply with the number of hours, such as *waa-Hida* for one o'clock. In Arabic the 12-hour clock is typically used, with the context usually being enough to know whether the speaker is referring to the morning or the evening. If you are asked a question which requires you to distinguish between morning and evening, then you would say *waa-Hida Sabaa-Han* (one in the morning), *waH-da Zoh-ran* (one in the afternoon) or *al-saa-biAa ma-saa 'an* (seven in the evening).

Some informal expressions
السَّاعة اثْنين بالضَّبط *fee al-saa-Aa it-nayn beZ-ZabT* at 2 o'clock on the dot
السَّاعة دلوقت ثمانية وشوية *al-saa-Aa al-aan al-thaa-mina wa sho-way-ya*
it's just gone 8 o'clock

The basics

early   مبكِّراً *mobak-kiran*

half an hour	نصف ساعة neSf saa-Aa
in the afternoon	بعد الظُّهر baAd al-dhohr
in the morning	في الصَّباح fee al-Sa-baaH
late	متأخِّر mota' kh-khir
midday	وقت الظُّهر waqt al-dhohr
midnight	مُنتصف اللَّيل mon-taSaf al-layl
on time	في الوقت المُحدَّد fee al-waqt al-mo-Had-dad
quarter of an hour	رُبع ساعة robA saa-Aa
three quarters of an hour	ثلاث أرباع السّاعة tha-laath ar-baA al-saa-Aa

Expressing yourself

what time is it?

كَمُ السّاعة الآن؟
kam al-saa-Aa al-aan?

excuse me, have you got the time, please?

من فضلك! كَمُ السّاعة الآن؟
min faD-lak, kam al-saa-Aa al-aan?

it's exactly three o'clock

السّاعة الآن الثّالثة بالضبط
al-saa-Aa al-aan al-thaa-le-tha bel-DabT

it's nearly one o'clock

الساعة الآن الواحدة تقريباً
al-saa-Aa al-aan al-waa-Hida taq-ree-ban

it's ten past one

الساعة الآن الواحدة وعشر دقائق
al-saa-Aa al-aan al-waa-Hidawa Ashr da-qaa-'iq

it's a quarter past one

الساعة الآن الواحدة والرُّبع
al-saa-Aa al-aan al-waa-Hida wa al-robA

it's a quarter to one

السّاعة الآن الواحدة إلا ربع
al-saa-Aa al-aan al-waa-Hida il-la robA

it's twenty past twelve

الساعة الآن الثانية عشرة و ثلث

al-saa-Aa al-aan al-thaa-ne-ya Aash-ra wa tholth

it's twenty to twelve

الساعة الآن الثانية عشرة إلا ثلث

al-saa-Aa al-aan al-thaa-ne-ya Aash-ra il-la tholth

it's half past one

السَّاعة الآن الواحِدة ونِصف

al-saa-Aa al-aan al-waa-Hida wa neSf

I arrived at about two o'clock

وصلتُ حوالي السَّاعة الثَّانية

wa-Salt Ha-waa-lee al-saa-Aa al-thaa-ne-ya

I set my alarm for nine

ضبطتُ المُنَبّه علي السَّاعة التّاسعة

DabaT-To al-monab-bih Ala al-saa-Aa al-taa-se-Aa

I waited twenty minutes

انتظرتُ عِشْرين دقيقة

in-taZar-to Aesh-reen da-qee-qa

the train was fifteen minutes late

تأخّر القِطارُ خَمْس عشْرة دقيقة

ta'akh-khar al-qe-Taar khams Aash-rat da-qee-qa

I got home an hour ago

وصلتُ المنزل منذ ساعة

wa-Salt al-man-zil mondh saa-Aa

shall we meet in half an hour?

هل نتقابل بعد نِصف ساعة؟

hal nataqaa-bal baAd neSf saa-Aa?

I'll be back in a quarter of an hour

سأعودُ بعد رُبع ساعة

sa-Aood baAd robA saa-Aa

there's a three-hour time difference between … and …

هناك ثلاث ساعات فَرْق توقيت بين ... و ...

hu-naak tha-laath saa-Aaat farq tow-qeet bayn … wa …

Understanding

يُغادِر كلَّ ساعة وكلَّ نصف ساعة
yoghaa-dir koll saa-Aa wa koll neSf saa-Aa
departs on the hour and the half-hour

مفتوح من السَّاعة العاشرة صباحاً إلى السَّاعة الرَّابعة بعد الظُّهر
maf-tooH min al-saa-Aa al-Aaa-shira Sa-baa-Han ila al-saa-Aa al-raa-biAa baAad al-Zohr
open from 10am to 4pm

يُعْرَض في السَّاعة السَّابعة مساء كل يوم
yoA-raD fee al-saa-Aa al-saa-biAa masaa-an koll yawm
it's on every evening at seven

يَستغرق حوالي سَّاعة ونصف
yastagh-riq Ha-waa-lee saa-Aa wa neSf
it lasts around an hour and a half

يفتح السَّاعة العاشرة صباحاً
yaf-taH al-saa-Aa al-Aaa-shira Sa-baa-Han
it opens at ten in the morning

NUMBERS

NUMBERS

0 صفر Sifr
1 واحد waa-Hid
2 اثنان ith-nan
3 ثلاثة thala-tha
4 أربعة ar-baAa
5 خمسة kham-sa
6 ستة sit-ta
7 سبعة sab-Aa
8 ثمانية thama-neya
9 تسعة tes-Aa
10 عشرة Aash-ra
11 أحد عشر aHad-Aashar
12 اثنا عشر ithna-Aashar
13 ثلاثة عشر tha-lath Aashar
14 أربعة عشر ar-baA Aashar
15 خمسة عشر khams-Aashar
16 ستة عشر sit-Aashar
17 سبعة عشر sabA-Aashar
18 ثمانية عشر tha-mane-Aashar
19 تسعة عشر tisA-Aashar
20 عشرون Aesh-roon
21 واحد وعشرون wa-Hid wa Aesh-roon
22 اثنان وعشرون eth-nan wa Aesh-roon
30 ثلاثون thala-thoon
35 خمس وثلاثون khams wa thala-thoon

40 أربعون ar-ba-Aoon
50 خمسون kham-soon
60 ستون sit-toon
70 سبعون sab-Aoon
80 ثمانون thama-noon
90 تسعون tis-Aoon
100 مائة ma-'ah
101 مائة وواحد ma-'ah wa waa-Hid
200 مائتين ma-'atayn
500 خمسمائة khams ma-'ah
1000 ألف alf
2000 ألفين al-fayn
10000 عشرة آلاف Aash-rat aa-laaf
1000000 مائة ألف ma-'at alf

first أول aw-wal
second ثان thaanee
third ثالث thaa-lith
fourth رابع raa-biA
fifth خامس khaa-mis
sixth سادس saa-dis
seventh سابع saa-biA
eighth ثامن thaa-min
ninth تاسع taa-siA
tenth عاشر Aaa-shir
twentieth العشرون al-Aesh-roon

20 plus 3 equals 23
عشرون زائد ثلاثة يساوي ثلاثة وعشرون
Aesh-roon za-'ed thala-tha yo-saa-wee thala-tha wa Aesh-roon

20 minus 3 equals 17
عشرون ناقص ثلاث يساوي سبعة عشر
Aesh-roon naa-qiS thala-tha yo-saa-wee sab-Aat Aashar

20 multiplied by 4 equals 80

عشرون فى أربعة يساوى ثمانون

Aesh-roon fee ar-baAa yo-saa-wee thama-noon

20 divided by 4 equals 5

عشرون على أربعة يساوى خمسة

Aesh-roon Ala ar-baAa yo-saa-wee kham-sa

DICTIONARY

ENGLISH-ARABIC DICTIONARY

able: to be able to قادر علي *qaa-dir Ala*

about عن *Aan* ; **to be about to do** علي وشك *Aala washak*

above فوق *fooq*

abroad في الخارج *fee al-khaa-rij*

accept يقبل *yaq-bal*

access منفذ *mondh* **130**

accident حادث *Haa-dith* **40, 129**

accommodation تكييف *tak-yeef*

across عبر *Aabr*

adaptor محول *moHow-wel*

address عنوان *Aon-waan*

admission دخول *do-khool*

advance: in advance سلفاً *salafan*

advice نصيحة *na-See-Ha*; **to ask someone's advice** يطلب نصيحة *yaT-lob na-See-Ha*

advise ينصح *yan-saH*

aeroplane طائرة *Taa-'e-ra*

after فيما بعد *fee-ma baAd*

afternoon فترة *fat-ra*

after-sun (cream) بعد حمام الشمس *baAd Ham-maam al-shams*

again مرة ثانية *mar-ra thaa-nay-ya*

against ضد *Did*

age عمر *Aomr*

air هواء *ha-waa*

air conditioning مكيف الهواء *mokay-yef al-ha-waa*

airline شركة طيران *sharikat Taya-raan*

airmail بريد جوي *ba-reed jow-wee*

airport مطار *maTaar*

alarm clock منبه *monab-bih*

alcohol كحول *ko-Holl*

Algeria الجزائر *al-jazaa-'ir*

alive حي/حيّه *Hayy/Hayy-ya*

all طول *Tool*; **all day** طول اليوم *Tool al-yawm*; **all week** طول الأسبوع *Tool al-os-booA*; **all the better** *moA-Zam*; **all the same** كلهم سواء *kol-lohom sa-waa'*; **all the time** طول الوقت *Tool al-waqt*; **all inclusive** شامل كل التكاليف *shaa-mil al-taka-leef*

allergic حساسية *Hasa-say-ya* **124, 126**

almost تقريبا *taq-ree-ban*

already بالفعل *bel-fiAl*

also أيضا *ay-Dan*

although رغم أن *raghma-ann*

always دائما *daa-'eman*

ambulance إسعاف *es-Aaaf* **121**

American أمريكية/أمريكية *am-ree-ke* (m)/*am-ree-kay-ya* (f)

among بين *bayna*

anaesthetic مخدر *mokhad-dir*

and و *wa*

animal حيوان *Haya-waan*

ankle كاحل *kaa-Hil*

anniversary ذكرى *dhik-raa*

another آخر *aa-khar*

answer (n) إجابة ejaa-ba
answer (v) يجيب yo-jeeb
answering machine جهاز استقبال المكالمات je-haaz is-tiq-baal al-mokaa-lamaat
ant نملة nam-la
antibiotics مضادة حيوي modaaD Haya-wee
anybody, anyone أي أحد ayy aHad
anything أي شيء ayy shay'
anyway على أي حال Aala ayy Haal
appendicitis إلتهاب الزائدة الدودية il-tihaab al-zaa-'ida al-doo-day-ya
appointment موعد mow-Aed'; **to make an appointment** يحدد موعد yo-Had-did mow-Aed 120; **to have an appointment with** لديه موعد مع laday-he mow-Aed maAa 122
April أبريل، نيسان ab-reel, ne-saan
area منطقة man-Tiqa; **in the area** في المنطقة fee al-man-Tiqa
arm ذراع dhe-raaA
around حول Haw-la
arrange يرتب yo-rat-tib; **to arrange to meet** يرتب موعد لمقابلة yo-rat-tib
arrival وصول wo-Sool
arrive يصل ya-Sil
art فن fann
artist فنّان/فنّانة fan-naan (m)/fann-naa-na (f)
as بينما bay-nama; **as soon as possible** بأسرع ما يمكن be-asraA ma yom-kin; **as soon as** بمجرد be-mojar-rad; **as well as** أيضاً ay-dan
ashtray طفاية سجاير Taf-faayat sajaa-yir
ask يسأل، يطلب yas-'al, yaTlob; **to ask a question** يسأل سؤال yas-'al

so-'aal
aspirin أسبرين as-be-reen
asthma ربو raboo
at في fee
attack (v) هجوم ho-joom 130
August أغسطس – آب oghos-Tos
autumn فصل خريف faSl al-kha-reef
available متاح motaaH
avenue طريق Ta-reeq
away: 10 km away بعيداً من هنا ba-Aeed min hu-na

B

baby طفل/طفلة Tifl (m)/Tifla (f)
baby's bottle رضّاعة الأطفال raD-DaaAat aT-faal
back خلف khalf; **at the back of** خلف khalf
backpack شنطة الظهر shan-Tat Zahr
bad سيء say-yi'; **it's not bad** ليس سيء lay-sa say-yi'
bag حقيبة Ha-qeeba
baggage شنط shonaT
Bahrain البحرين al-baH-rayn
bake يخبز yakh-bez
baker's مخبز makh-baz
balcony شرفة shor-fa
bandage ضمادة Dam-maa-Da
bank بنك bank 105
banknote ورقة نقدية waraqa naq-day-ya
bar بار baar
barbecue حفل شواء Hafl sho-waa
bath حمّام Ham-maam; **to have a bath** يستحم/تستحم yas-ta-Him (m)/tas-ta-Him (f)
bath towel فوطة حمّام foo-Tat Ham-maam

bathroom غرفة حمّام ghor-fat Ham-maam

battery بطّارية baT-Taa-ray-ya **40**

be يكون/تكون yakoon/takoon

beach شاطئ shaa-Ti'

beach umbrella شمسية بحر shal-say-yat baHr

beard لحية leh-ya

beautiful جميل ja-meel

because لأن le-'an-na; **because of** بسبب be-sabab

bed سرير sa-reer

bee نحلة naH-la

before من قبل min qabl

begin بدأ bada'

beginner مبتدئ/مبتدئة mob-tade'

beginning بداية be-daa-ya'; **at the beginning** في البداية fee al-be-daa-ya

behind خلف khalf

believe يعتقد yaA-taqid

below تحت taHt

beside بجانب be-jaa-nib

best أفضل af-Dal; **the best** الأفضل al-af-Dal

better أفضل af-Dal; **to get better** يتحسن yata-Has-san; **it's better to …** من الأفضل أن … min al-af-Dal ann …

between بين bayna

bicycle درّاجة dar-raa-ja

bicycle pump منفاخ الدرّاجة min-faakh al-dar-raa-ja

big كبير/كبيرة ka-beer/ka-bee-ra

bike دراجة dar-raa-ja

bill فاتورة fa-tora **59**

bin سلّة المهملات sal-lat al-moh-malaat

binoculars منظار مكبر min-Zaar mokab-bir

birthday عيد ميلاد Aeed mee-laad

bit لقمة loq-ma

bite (n) عضة AaD-Da

bite (v) يعض ya-AoD

black أسود as-wad

blackout تعتيم taA-teem

blanket بطّانية baT-Taa-nay-ya

bleed ينزف yan-zif

blind أعمى aA-ma

blister بثرة bath-ra

blood دم damm

blood pressure ضغط دم DaghT damm

blue زرقاء zar-qaa'

board لوح lowH

boarding الضيافة al-De-yaa-fa

boat قارب qaa-rib

body جسم jism

book (n) كتاب ke-taab; **book of tickets** دفتر التذاكر daf-tar al-ta-dhaa-kir

book (v) يحجز yaH-jiz

bookshop مكتبة mak-taba

boot (of car) شنطة shan-Ta

borrow يقترض yaq-tariD

botanical garden حديقة نباتات Ha-dee-qat naba-taat

both كل من kol-lan min; **both of us** أنا وأنت ana wa an-ta

bottle زجاجة zojaa-ja

bottle opener فتّاحة زجاجات fat-taa-Hat zojaa-jaat

bottom قاع qaaA; **at the bottom** في القاع fee al-qaaA; **at the bottom of** في قاع fee qaaA

bowl قصعة qaS-Aa

bra سوتيانة sot-yaa-na

brake (n) فرامل faraa-mil

brake (v) يدوس على الفرامل ya-doos Ala al-faraa-mil

bread خبز *khobz*

break يكسر *yak-sar*; **to break one's leg** يكسر ساقه *yak-sar saa-qo*

break down يتعطّل *yata-AaT-Tal* **130**

breakdown عطل *AoTl*

breakdown service خدمة أعطال السيّارات *khed-mat aA-Taal al-say-ya-raat*

breakfast إفطار *if-Taar* **47**; **to have breakfast** يتناول الإفطار *yatana-wal al-if-Taar*

bridge جسر *jisr*

bring يُحضر *yoH-Dir*

brochure كراسة التفاصيل *kor-raa-sat al-mowa-Safaat*

broken مكسور *mak-soor*

bronchitis نزلة شعبيّة *naz-la shoAa-bay-ya*

brother أخ *akh*

brown بُنّي *bon-nee*

brush فرشاة *for-sha*

build يبني *yab-nee*

building مبنى *mab-naa*

bump يصدم *yaS-dom*

bumper إكسدام *iks-daam*

buoy عوامة *Aow-waa-ma*

burn (n) حرق *Harq*

burn (v) يحرق *yaH-riq*; **to burn oneself** يحرق نفسه/تحرق نفسها *yah-riq naf-so taH-riq naf-saha*

burst (n) إنفجار *infe-jaar*

burst (v) ينفجر *yan-fajir*

bus أتوبيس *oto-bees* **37**

bus route مسار الأتوبيس *masaar al-oto-bees*

bus station موقف أتوبيس *mow-qaf oto-bees*

bus stop محطّة أتوبيس *maHa-TaT*

oto-bees

busy مشغول/مشغولة *mash-ghool* (m)/*mash-ghoola* (f)

but لكن *la-kin*

butcher's محل جزارة *maHal ji-zaa-ra*

buy يشتري *yash-ta-ree*

by بـ *be*; **by car** بالسيارة *bel-say-ya-ra*

bye! مع السلامة *maAa al-salaa-ma*

C

café مقهى *maq-ha*

call (n) مكالمة *mokaa-lama*

call (v) يتصل *yat-taSil*; **to be called** يتلقى اتصال *yatalaq-qa it-te-Saal*

call back يعاود الإتّصال/يعود فيما بعد *yo-Aaa-wed al-it-te-Saal/ya-Aood fee-ma baAd* **116**

camel جمل *jamal*

camera كاميرا *camera*

camper ساكن الخيام *saa-kin al-khe-yaam*

camping إقامة في مخيم *iqaa-ma fee mokhay-yam*; **to go camping** يذهب للإقامة في مخيم *yadh-hab lil-iqaa-ma fee mokhay-yam*

camping stove موقد مخيم *mow-qid mokhay-yam*

campsite مكان المخيم *makaan mokhay-yam*

can (n) علبة *Aol-ba*

can (v) يستطيع/تستطيع *yasta-TeeA/tasta-TeeA*; **I can't** انا لا أستطيع *ana la asta-TeeA*

can opener فتّاحة علب *fat-taa-Hat Aolab*

cancel يلغي *yal-ghe*

candle شمعة sham-Aa
car سيارة say-ya-ra
car park موقف سيارات mow-qaf say-ya-raat
caravan سيَّارة سكنية say-ya-ra saka-nay-ya
card بطاقة be-Taa-qa
carry يحمل yaH-mil
case: in case of حالة Haa-la
cash نقود no-qood; **to pay cash** يدفع نقداً yad-faA naq-dan **94**
cashpoint ماكينة صرَّاف الي makee-nat Sar-raaf aa-lee **105**
catch يمسك yom-sik
CD سي دي see-dee
cemetery مقابر maqaa-bir
centimetre سنتيمتر sante-metr
centre مركز mar-kaz
century قرن qarn
chair كرسي kor-see
change (n) (money) تغيير tagh-yeer **94**
change (v) يغير yo-ghay-yer **105**
changing room غرفة القياس ghor-fat al-qe-yaas **97**
channel قناة qanaa
charge (n) تكلفة tak-lifa
charge (v) يكلف yo-kal-lif
cheap رخيص ra-kheeS
check تدقيق tad-qeeq
check in يفحص الاوراق عند الدخول yaf-HaS al-awraaq Aenda al-do-khool **34**
check-in فحص الاوراق عند الدخول faHS al-awraaq Aenda al-do-khool
checkout الدفع والمغادرة al-dafA wa al-moghaa-dara
cheers! في صحتك fee SiH-Hitak
chemist's صيدلية Say-da-lay-ya

cheque شيك sheek
chest صدر Sadr
child طفل/طفلة Tifl (m)/Tifla (f)
chilly بارد baa-rid
chimney مدخنة mad-khana
chin ذقن dhaqn
church كنيسة ka-neesa
cigar سيجار see-gaar
cigarette سيجارة see-gara
cigarette paper ورق لف سجاير waraq laff saga-yir
cinema سينما cinema
circus سيرك sirk
city مدينة madee-na
clean (adj) نظيف na-Zeef
clean (v) ينظف yo-naZ-Zif
cliff جرف jorf
climate مناخ manaakh
climbing تسلق tasal-loq
cloakroom حجرة إيداع المعاطف Hoj-rat ee-daaA al-maAaa-Tif
close (v) يغلق yogh-liq
closed مغلق mogh-laq
closing time ميعاد الغلق mi-Aaad al-ghalq
clothes ملابس malaa-bis
clutch قابض qaa-biD
coach حافلة Haa-fila
coast ساحل saa-Hil
coathanger شماعة الملابس sham-maa-Aa
cockroach صرصار Sor-Saar
coffee قهوة qah-wa
coil (contraceptive) لولب low-lab
coin عملة Aom-la
Coke® كولا cola
cold (n) برد bard; **to have a cold** يصاب بنزلة برد yo-Saab be-nazlat bard
cold (adj) بارد baa-rid; **it's cold** الجو

بارد al-jow baa-rid; **I'm cold** اشعر بالبرد ashAor bil-bard

collection جميع taj-meeA

colour لون lown

comb مشط mishT

come يأتي ya'-tee

come back يعود ya-Aood

come in يدخل yad-khol

come out يخرج yakh-roj

comfortable مريح mo-reeH

company شركة sharika

compartment جويف taj-weef

complain يشتكي yash-takee

comprehensive insurance تأمين شامل ta'-meen shaa-mil

computer حاسوب Haa-soob

concert حفل موسيقي Hafl moo-see-qe

concert hall قاعة الحفلات الموسيقية qaa-Aat al-Hafa-laat al-moo-see-qay-ya

concession تخفيض takh-feeD 32, 80

condom عازل طبي Aaa-zil Tib-bee

confirm يؤكد yo'ak-kid 34

connection إتصال it-te-Saal 34

constipated لديه حالة إمساك laday-he Haa-lat im-saak

consulate قنصلية qonSo-lay-ya 129

contact (n)أحد المعارف aHad al-maAaa-rif

contact (v) ينتصل ب yat-taSil be

contact lenses عدسات لاصقة Aada-saat laa-Siqa

contagious معدي moA-dee

contraceptive مانع للحمل maa-niA lil-Haml

cook (v) يطبخ yaT-bokh

cooked مطبوخ maT-bookh

cooking طبيخ Ta-beekh; **to do the cooking** يقوم بالطبخ yaqoom bel-Tabkh

cool بارد baa-rid

Coptic قبطي qib-Tee

corkscrew لولب نزع فلين الزجاجات low-lab le-nazA fel-leen al-zojaa-jaat

correct صحيح Sa-HeeH

cost تكلفة tak-lefa

cotton قطن qoTn

cotton bud قطن تنظيف الأذن qoTn tan-Zeef al-odhon

cough (n) كحة koH-Ha; **to have a cough** يعاني من الكحة yo-Aaa-nee min al-koH-Ha

cough (v) يكح yakoH

count يحسب yaH-sib

country بلد balad

countryside ريف reef

course: of course بالطبع bel-TabA

cover (n) غطاء ghiTaa'

cover (v) يغطي yoghaT-Tee

credit card بطاقة إئتمان be-Taa-qat e'-ti-maan 45, 94

cross (n)صليب Sa-leeb

cross (v)يعبر yaA-bor

cruise رحلة بحرية riHla baHaray-ya

cup فنجان fin-jaan

currency عملة Aom-la

customs عادات Aaa-daat

cut يقطع yaq-TaA; **to cut oneself** يعزل نفسه عن yaA-zil naf-so Aan

cycle path طريق لسير الدرّاجات Ta-reeq sayr al-dar-ra-jaat

D

damaged متضرر motaDar-rir

damp رطوبة ro-Tooba

dance (n) رقص raqS

dance (v) يرقص yar-qoS

dangerous خطر khaTar

dark مظلم moz-lim; **dark blue** أزرق داكن azraq daa-kin

date (n) تاريخ taa-reekh; **out of date** منتهي الصلاحية montahee al-Salaa-Hay-ya

date from يبدأ من yab-da' min

date of birth تاريخ الميلاد taa-reekh al-mee-laad

daughter ابنة ebnah

day يوم yawm; **the day after tomorrow** بعد غد baAd ghadd; **the day before yesterday** امس الأول ams al-aw-wal

dead ميت may-yet

deaf أصم aSamm

dear عزيز Aazeez

debit card بطاقة الدفع be-Taa-qat al-dafA

December ديسمبر dee-samber, كانون الأول kaanon al-aw-wal

declare يعلن yoA-len

deep عميق Aameeq

degree درجة daraja

delay تأخير ta'-kheer

delayed متأخر mota'akh-khir

deli محل أطعمة الخاصة maHal aT-Aema khaaS-Sa

dentist طبيب أسنان Tabeeb as-naan

deodorant مزيل رائحة العرق mo-zeel raa-'iHat al-Aaraq

department قسم qism

department store محل متعدد الأقسام maHal motaAad-did al-aqsaam

departure مغادرة moghaa-dara

depend: that depends on يعتمد على yaA-tamid Aala

deposit تأمين ta'-meen

dessert طبق الحلو Tabaq al-Helo 57

develop: to get a film developed يحمّض yoHam-miD 101

diabetes داء السكري daa' al-sok-karee

dialling code رقم raqam

diarrhoea: to have diarrhoea إسهال is-Haal

die يموت yamoot

diesel ديزل dee-zel

different مختلف mokh-talif

difficult صعب SaAb

digital camera كاميرا رقمية camera raqamay-ya

dinner العشاء al-aashaa'; **to have dinner** يتناول طعام العشاء yatanaa-wal TaAam al-Ashaa'

direct مباشر mobaashir

direction اتجاه it-tijaah

directory دليل daleel

directory enquiries إستعلامات الدليل is-tiA-la-maat al-daleel

dirty (adj) قذر qadhir

disabled معاق moAallaq

disaster كارثة kaa-ritha

disco ديسكو disco

discount تخفيض takh-feeD 80; **to give someone a discount** يعطي تخفيض yoA-Tee takh-feeD

discounted fare أجرة مخفضة ojra mokhaf-faDa

dish طبق Tabaq

dishes اطباق aTbaaq; **to do the dishes** يغسل الأطباق yaghsil al-aTbaaq

dish towel فوطة تجفيف الأطباق foo-Tat taj-feef al-aTbaaq

dishwasher غسالة أطباق ghassaalat aTbaaq

disinfect يعقّم yoAaq-qim

disposable للإستخدام مرة واحدة lil-is-tikh-daam mar-ra waa-Hida

disturb يزعج yoz-Aej; **do not disturb** لا تسبب إزعاج la tosabib ez-Aaaj

dive غطس ghaTs

diving: to go diving الغوص al-ghowS

do هل hal; **do you have a light?** هل معك كبريت؟ hal maAaka kab-reet?

doctor دكتور / دكتورة dok-toor (m)/ dok-too-ra (f) **120**

door باب baab

door code كود فتح الباب kood fatH al-baab

downstairs الطابق الأسفل al-Taa-biq al-asfal

dress: to get dressed يرتدي الملابس yar-tadee al-malaa-bis

dressing ضمّادة Dam-maa-Da

drink (n) مشروب mashroob; **to go for a drink** يخرج لتناول مشروب yakh-roj le-tanaa-wol mashroob **54**; **to have a drink** يتناول مشروب yatana-wal mashroob

drink (v) يشرب yashrab

drinking water ماء شرب maa' shorb

drive: (n) **to go for a drive** نزهة بالسيّارة nozha bil-say-ya-ra

drive (v) يقود yaqood

driving licence رخصة قيادة rokh-Sat qe-yaa-da

drops قطرة qaT-ra

drown يغرق yagh-raq

drugs أدوية ad-way-ya

drunk سكران/سكرانة sak-raan

(m)/sak-raa-na (f)

dry (adj) جاف jaaf

dry (v) يجفف yojaf-fif

dry cleaner's محل التنظيف الجاف للملابس maHal al-tanzeef al-jaaf lil-malaa-bis

during خلال khe-laal; **during the week** خلال الأسبوع khe-laal al-os-booA

dustbin صندوق القمامة Son-dooq qe-maama

duty chemist's صيدلية الخدمة الليلية Say-da-lay-ya al-khid-ma al-lay-lay-ya

E

each كل koll

ear أذن odhon

early مبكرا mobak-kiran

earplugs سدادات الأذن sada-daat al-odhon

earrings حلقان Hil-qaan

earth أرض arD

east شرق sharq; **in the east** من الشرق mina al-sharq; **(to the) east of** ناحية الشرق naa-Heyat al-sharq

Easter عيد الفصح Aeed al-fiSH

easy سهل sahl

eat يأكل ya'-kol **54**

economy class درجة عادية daraja Aaa-deya

Egypt مصر maSr

electric كهربائية kahraba-'eya

electric shaver ماكينة حلاقة كهربائية makee-nat He-laaqa kahraba-'ceya

electricity كهرباء kahrabaa'

electricity meter عداد كهرباء Aad-daad kahrabaa'

e-mail بريد الكتروني ba-reed elek-troo-nee

e-mail address عنوان البريد الالكتروني Aon-waan al-ba-reed al-elek-troo-nee 25, 111

embassy سفارة sefaa-ra

emergency طوارئ Ta-waa-re' 129

emergency exit مخرج طوارئ makh-raj Ta-waa-re'

empty فارغ faa-righ

end نهاية ne-haa-ya; **at the end of** في نهاية fee ne-haa-yat; **at the end of the street** عند اخر الشارع Aenda aa-khir al-shaa-riA

engaged مشغول mash-ghool

engine محرك moHar-rik

England انجلترا in-gel-tera

English إنجليزي/إنجليزية in-glee-ze (m)/in-glee-zay-ya (f)

enjoy: enjoy your meal! بالهنا والشفا bel-hana wa al-shefa; **to enjoy oneself** يستمتع بوقته yastam-tiA be-waqto

enough كاف ka-fe; **that's enough** هذا يكفي ha-dha yak-fe

entrance مدخل mad-khal

envelope مظروف maZ-roof

epileptic مصاب بالصرع moSaab bel-SaraA

equipment جهاز ji-jaaz

Eurocheque شيك سياحي باليورو sheek se-yaa-He bel-yoo-ro

Europe أوروبا o-rob-ba

European أوروبي o-rob-be (m)/o-rob-bay-ya (f)

evening مساء masaa'; **in the evening** في المساء fee al-masaa'

every كل koll; **every day** كل يوم koll yawm

everybody, **everyone** كل شخص koll shakhS

everywhere في كل مكان fee koll makaan

except ماعدا ma Aada

exceptional استثنائي ith-tith-naa-'e

excess فائض faa-'eD

exchange تغيير tagh-yeer

exchange rate نسبة التغيير nesbat al-tagh-yeer

excuse (n) عذر Aodhr

excuse: (v) **excuse me** من فضلك min faD-lak

exhaust عادم Aaa-dim

exhausted منهك mon-hak

exhaust pipe ماسورة العادم maa-sorat al-Aaa-dim

exhibition معرض maA-raD 79

exit مخرج makh-raj

expensive غالي gha-lee

expiry date تاريخ إنتهاء الصلاحية taa-reekh in-tihaa' al-Salaa-Hay-ya

express (adj) سريع sa-reeA

expresso قهوة إسبرسو qah-wa expresso

extra إضافي e-Daa-fee

eye عين Aayn

F

face وجه wajh

facecloth فوطة الوجه foo-Tat al-wajh

fact حقيقة Haqee-qa; **in fact** في الواقع fee al-waa-qiA

fall (v) يسقط yas-qoT; **to fall asleep** ينام من التعب yanaam min al-taAab; **to fall ill** يصاب بالمرض yoSaab bel-maraD

family أسرة os-raa
fan مروحة mar-waHa
far بعيد ba-Aeed; **far from** بعيد عن ba-Aeed Aan
fare أجرة ojra
fast سريع sa-reeA
fast-food restaurant مطعم الوجبات الجاهزة maT-Aam al-waj-baat al-jaa-hiza
fat سمين sameen
father أب ubb
favour معروف maA-roof; **to do someone a favour** يصنع معروف لـ yaSnaA maA-roof li
favourite شيء مفضل shay' mofaD-dal
fax فاكس fax
February فبراير febra-yir, شباط shibaaT
feel يشعر yash-Aor; **to feel good** يشعر بالسرور yash-Aor bil-so-roor; **to feel bad** يشعر بعدم الرضا yash-Aor be-Aadam al-riDa
feeling إحساس iH-saas
ferry عبّارة Aab-bara
festival مهرجان mahra-jaan
fetch يجلب yaj-lib
fever حمى Hom-ma; **to have a fever** يصاب بالحمى yoSaab bel-Hom-ma
few قليل qaleel
fiancé خطيب khaTeeb
fiancée خطيبة khaTee-ba
fight شجار shi-jaar
fill يملأ yam-la'
fill in يشغل وظيفة yash-ghal wa-Zee-fa
fill out يملأ نموذج yam-la' namoo-zaj
fill up: to fill up with petrol يملأ

by yam-la' al-tank bil-kaa-mil يملأ التنك بالكامل
filling (in tooth) حشو Hashoo
film فيلم film 101
finally أخيرا akhee-ran
find يجد yajid
fine (n) غرامة gharaa-ma
fine (adj) جيد jay-yid; **I'm fine** أنا بخير ana be-kheir
finger إصبع is-baA
finish ينهي/ينتهي yon-hee/yan-tahee
fire نار naar, حريق Ha-reeq
fire brigade المطافي al-maTaa-fee
fireworks ألعاب نارية al-Aaab naa-ray-ya
first أولا aw-walan
first class درجة أولى daraja oo-laa
first floor الطابق الأول al-Taa-biq al-aw-wal
first name الإسم الأول al-ism al-aw-wal
fish (n) سمكة samaka
fish shop محل اسماك maHal asmaak
fitting room غرفة القياس gho-fat al-qe-yaas
fizzy فوّار faw-waar
flash فلاش flash
flask قارورة qa-roo-ra
flat (adj) مسطح mosaT-TaH
flat (n) شقّة shaq-qa
flavour نكهة nak-ha
flaw عيب Aayb
flight رحلة riHla
floor: on the floor على الأرض Aala al-arD; **ground floor** الطابق الأرضي al-Taa-biq al-ar-Dee
flu إنفلونزا influ-wan-za
fly (n) حشرة طائرة hashara
fly (v) يطير ya-Teer
food طعام Ta-Aaam

food poisoning تسمم غذائي Tasam-mom

foot قدم qadam

for لِ le

forbidden ممنوع mam-nooA

forecast توقع tawaq-qoA

forehead جبين Ja-been

foreign أجنبي aj-nabe

foreigner أجنبي/أجنبية aj-nabe (m)/aj-na-bay-ya (f)

forest غابة ghaa-ba

fork شوكة sho-ka

former سابق saa-beq

forward (adj) إلي الأمام ila al-amaam

four-star petrol بنزين متاز ban-zeen mom-taaz

fracture كسور ko-soor

fragile قابل للكسر qaa-bil lil-kasr

free غير مشغول ghayr mash-ghool

Friday يوم الجمعة yawm al-jumAa

fridge ثلاجة thal-laa-ja

fried مقلي maq-lee

friend صديقة/صديق Sa-deeq (m)/Sa-dee-qa (f)

from من min

front مقدمة moqad-dima

fry يقلي yaq-lee

frying pan مقلاة maq-laah

full تام kaa-mil

full board إقامة كاملة iqaa-ma kaa-mila

full fare, full price أجرة كاملة/سعر كامل ojra kaa-mila/siAr kaa-mil

fuse منصهر mon-Sahir

G

gallery معرض maA-rad

game لعبة loA-ba

garage جراج garage **39**

garden حديقة Hadee-qa

gas غاز ghaaz

gas cylinder أسطوانة غاز os-Towaa-nat ghaaz

gastric flu حمى معوية Hom-ma maAaway-ya

gate بوابة baw-waa-ba

gay يميل الي الجنس المماثل yameel ila al-jins al-momaa-thil

gearbox صندوق غيار السرعة Son-dooq ghe-yaar al-sorAa

general عام Aaam

gents' (toilet) حمّام الرجال Ham-maam al-re-jaal

get علي يحصل yaH-Sol Aala

get off ينزل yan-zil

get up يستيقظ yastay-qiZ

gift wrap الهدايا ورق للف waraq lil-laff al-hadaa-ya

girl بنت bint

girlfriend رفيقة ra-feeqa

give يعطي yoA-Tee

give back يعيد yo-Aeed

glass كأس ka'ss; **a glass of water** كأس من الماء ka'ss min al-maa'

glasses نظّارة naZ-Zaa-ra

gluten-free خالي من الجلوتين khaa-lee min al-glu-teen

go يذهب yadh-hab; **to go to Alexandria** الإسكندرية يسافر الي yosaa-fir ila al-iskanda-ray-ya; **we're going home tomorrow** سنعود الي بلدنا غداً sana-Aood ila bala-dina ghadan

go away يسافر الي yosaa-fir

go in يدخل yad-khol

go out يخرج yakh-roj

go with يخرج مع yakh-roj maAa

good الخير al-kheir; **good morning** صباح الخير Sa-baaH al-kheir; **good**

afternoon نهارك سعيد na-haarak sa-Aeed; **good evening** مساء الخير masaa' al-kheir

goodbye مع السلامة maAa al-salaa-ma

goodnight تصبح علي خير teSbaH Aala kheir

goods بضاعة baDaa-'eA

GP ممارس عام momaa-ris Aaam

grams جرام gram

grass عشب Aoshb

great عظيم Aa-Zeem

green أخضر akh-Dar

grey رمادي ramaa-dee

grocer's محل بقالة maHal be-qaa-la

ground أرض arD

ground floor الطابق الارضي al-Taa-biq al-ar-Dee

grow ينمو yan-moo

guarantee ضمان Damaan

guest ضيف/ضيفة Dayf (m)/Day-fa (f)

guide مرشد/مرشدة mor-shid (m)/ mor-shida (f)

guidebook دليل daleel

guided tour جولة مع مرشد jow-la maAa mor-shid

gynaecologist طبيب نساء tabeeb nisaa'

H

hair شعر shaAr

hairdresser حلّاق Hal-laaq

hairdrier مجفف الشعر mojaf-fif shaAr

half نصف neSf

half-kilo نصف كيلو neSf kilo

hand يد yadd

handbag حقيبة يد Ha-qee-ba

handbrake فرامل اليد fa-raa-mil al-yadd

handicapped معاق moAaaq

handkerchief منديل man-deel

hand luggage حقيبة اليد Ha-qee-bat yadd **34**

hand-made مصنوع يدوي maS-nooA yada-wee

happen يحدث yaH-doth

happy سعيد/سعيدة sa-Aeed (m)/sa-Aee-da (f)

hard صلب Salb

hashish حشيش Ha-sheesh

hat قبعة qob-baAa

hate يكره yak-rah

have يتناول yatana-wal

have to يضطر إلي yaD-Tarr ila

hay fever حمي القش Hom-ma al-qash

he هو hu-wa

head رأس ra'ss

headache: to have a headache عنده صداع Aan-do So-daaA

headlight مصباح أمامي meS-baaH amaa-mee

health صحة SeH-Ha

hear يسمع yas-maA

heart قلب qalb

heart attack أزمة قلبية azma qal-bay-ya

heat حرارة Ha-raa-ra

heating تدفئة tad-fi'a

heavy ثقيل tha-qeel

hello مرحبا mar-Haba

helmet خوذة khoo-dha

help (n) مساعدة mosaa-Aada; **to call for help** يطلب مساعدة yaT-lob mosaa-Aada; **help!** النجدة! al-naj-da!

help (v) يساعد yosaa-Aed **128**
her ها ha
here هنا hu-na; **here is/are** هذا ha-dha hu-wa/haa-olaa هوا/هؤلاء هم hom
hers خاص بها khaaS be-ha
hi! أهلا ah-lan
hi-fi هاي فاي hi-fi
high عال Aaa-le
high blood pressure ضغط دم عالي DaghT damm Aaa-lee
high tide مد madd
hiking رحلة سير riHlat sayr **85**
hill تل tal
him ـه oh
hip عظمة الفخذ AaZ-mat al-fakhdh
hire (n) اجرة ojra
hire (v) يستأجر yas-ta'-jir **40, 84, 87**
his ـه oh
hold يمسك yom-sik
hold on! (on the phone) إنتظر in-taZir
holiday(s) عطلة AoTla
home البيت al-bayt; **at home** بالبيت bil-bayt; **to go home** يذهب الي البيت yadh-hab ila al-bayt
homosexual مثلي الجنس mith-lee al-jins
honest صادق Saa-diq
honeymoon شهر عسل shahr Aasal
horse حصان HoSaan
hospital مستشفى mos-tashfa
hot حار Haar; **it's hot** الجو حار al-jow Haar; **hot drink** مشروب ساخن Mashroob saa-khin
hotel فندق fon-doq **47**
hotplate طبق ساخن Tabaq saa-khin
hour ساعة saa-Aa
house منزل man-zil
housework اعمال منزلية aA-maal

man-ze-lay-ya; **to do the housework** يقوم بالاعمال المنزلية yaqoom bil-aA-maal al-man-ze-lay-ya
how كيف keyfa
hunger جوع jooA
hungry: to be hungry جائعة jaa-'eA
hurry: to be in a hurry إستعجال is-tiA-jaal
hurry (up) بسرعة be-sorAa
hurt: it hurts يؤلم yo'-lim; **my head hurts** رأسي يؤلمني ra'-see yo'-lim-nee
husband زوج zawj

I

I أنا ana; **I'm English** أنا انجليزي ana in-glee-zee; **I'm 22 (years old)** عمري اثنان وعشرون عام ana Aom-ree ithnan wa Aeshroon Aam
ice جليد je-leed
identity card بطاقة الهوية be-Taa-qat al-ha-way-ya
identity papers اوراق الهوية aw-raaq al-ha-way-ya
if لو low
ill مريضة mare-Da
illness مرض maraD
important مهم mo-him
in في fee; **in Egypt** في مصر fee MiSr; **in 2007** في عام الفين وسبعة fee Aam al-fayn wa sabAa; **in Arabic** في اللغة العربية fee al-logha al-Aarabay-ya; **in the 19th century** في القرن التاسع عشر fee al-qarn al-taa-s-A Aashar; **in an hour** في خلال ساعة fee khe-lal saa-Aa

included شامل shaa-mil **47**, **50**, **60**

independent مستقل mos-taqil

indicator مؤشر mo'ash-shir

infection تلوث talow-woth

information معلومة maA-loma **78**

injection حقنة Hoqna

injured مجروح maj-rooH

insect حشرة Hashara

insecticide مبيد حشري mobeed Hasha-ree

inside داخل daa-khil

insomnia حالة أرق Haa-lat araq

instant coffee قهوة فورية qah-wa fow-ray-ya

instead بدلا من badalan min

insurance تأمين ta'-meen

intend to ينوي عمل yan-wee Aamal

international دولي dow-lee

international money order حوالة نقدية دولية He-waa-la naq-day-ya dow-lay-ya

Internet إنترنت internet

Internet café مقهى انترنت maq-ha internet **111**

invite يدعو yad-Aoo

Iraq العراق al-Aeraaq

iron (n) مكواة mak-wa

iron (v) يكوي yak-wee

Islamic إسلامي is-laa-mee

island جزيرة jazee-ra

it هو/هي hu-wa (m)/he-ya (f); **it's beautiful** هو جميل hu-wa ja-meel; **it's warm** الجو دافئ al-jow daa-fee

itchy: it's itchy بها حكة beha Hak-ka

item شيء shay'

jacket جاكت jaa-kit

January يناير ya-naa-yir, كانون الثاني ka-noon al-thaa-nee

jetlag إرهاق السفر ir-haaq al-safar

jeweller's محل صائغ maHal Saa-yigh

jewellery مجوهرات mojow-haraat

job عمل Aamal

jogging يعدو yaA-do

Jordan الأردن al-ordon

journey سفرية safaray-ya

jug إبريق eb-reeq

juice عصير Aa-Seer

July تموز yol-yoo, يوليو tam-mouz

jumper فانلة fa-nila

June يونيو yon-yoo, حزيران Hozay-raan

keep يحفظ yaH-faZ

key مفتاح mof-taaH **40**, **48**, **50**

kidney كلية kel-ya

kill يقتل yaq-tol

kilometre كيلومتر kilo-metr

kind: what kind of? نوع nooA

kitchen مطبخ maT-bakh

knee ركبة rok-ba

knife سكينة sek-keena

knock down يخبط yakh-baT

know يعرف yaA-rif

Kuwait الكويت al-ko-wayt

ladies' (toilet) حمام السيدات Ham-maam al-say-ye-daat

lake بحيرة boHay-ra

lamp مصباح moS-baaH

landmark مَعلَم maA-lam

landscape منظر طبيعي manZar

Tabee-Aee

language لغة *logha*

laptop الحاسوب المحمول *al-Ha-soob al-maH-mool*

last (adj) ماضي *maa-Dee*; **last year** العام الماضي *al-Aaam al-maa-Dee*

last (v) يظل *yaZal*

late متأخرا *mota'akh-khir*

late-night opening يعمل حتي وقت متأخر من الليل *yaA-mal Hat-ta waqt mota'akhi-khir min al-layl*

laugh يضحك *yaD-Hak*

launderette مغسلة *magh-sala*

lawyer محامي/محامية *moHaa-me* (m)/*moHa-may-ya* (f)

leaflet مطبوعة *maT-booAa*

leak يتسرب *yatasar-rub*

learn يتعلم *yataAal-lam*

least: the least أدني *adna*; **at least** علي الأقل *Ala al-aqal*

leave إذن *edhn*; يغادر *yoghaa-dir*

Lebanon لبنان *lib-naan*

left يسار *yasaar*; **to the left (of)** إلي ناحية اليسار من *ila al-yasaar min*

left-luggage (office) مكتب الحقائب المتروكة *mak-tab al-Haqaa-'ib al-matroo-ka*

leg ساق *saaq*

lend يسلّت *yosal-lif*

lens عدسة *Aadasa*

lenses عدسات *Aada-saat*

less أقل *aqal*; **less than.** أقل من. *aqal min*

let يترك/يؤجر *yat-rok*

letter خطاب *khe-Taab*

library مكتبة *mak-taba*

Libya ليبيا *leb-ya*

life حياة *Ha-yaah*

lift مصعد *miS-Aad*

light (adj) فاتح *faa-tiH*; **light blue**

أزرق فاتح *azraq faa-tiH*

light (n) ثقاب *thiqaab*; **do you have a light?** هل لديك كبريت؟ *hal laday-ka kab-reet?*

light (v) يشعل *yosh-Ail*

light bulb مصباح *meS-baaH*

lighter ولاعة *wal-laa-Aa*

lighthouse منارة *manaa-ra*

like (adv) مثل *mithl*

like (v) يريد *yo-reed*; **I'd like** أريد *ana o-reed*

line خط *khaTT*

lip شفة *shifaa*

listen يستمع *yas-tamiA*

litre لتر *litr*

little (adj) قليل *qa-leel*

little (adv) بقدر قليل *be-qadr qa-leel*

live حي *Hayy*

liver كبدة *kib-da*

living room غرفة المعيشة *ghor-fat al-ma-Aee-sha*

local time التوقيت المحلي *al-tow-qeet al-maHal-lee*

lock قفل *qifl*

long طويل *Ta-weel*; **a long time** منذ وقت طويل *mondh waqt ta-weel*; **how long... ?** ما مدة ... ؟ *ma mod-dat ...?*

look يبدو *yab-doo* **96**; **to look tired** يبدو مرهق *yab-doo mor-haqan*

look after ب يعتني *yaA-tanee be*

look at ينظر إلي *yanZor ila*

look for يبحث عن *yab-Hath*

look like يشبه *yosh-bih*

lose يفقد *yaf-qid* **40**; **to get lost** يتوه *ya-tooh*; **to be lost** فقد *foqid*

lot: a lot (of) كثير من *ka-theer min*

loud عالي *Aaa-lee*

low منخفض *mon-khafiD*

low blood pressure ضغط دم منخفض DaghT damm mon-khafiD

low-fat قليل الدسم qaleel al-dasam

low tide جزر jazr

luck حظ HaZZ

lucky: to be lucky محظوظ maH-ZooZ

luggage حقيبة Ha-qee-ba **34**

lunch غداء ghadhaa'; **to have lunch** يتناول الغداء yatana-wal al-ghazaa'

lung رئة re-'a

luxury (n) رغد raghad

luxury (adj) مُرفَه moraf-fah

M

magazine مجلة mejal-la

maiden name الإسم قبل الزواج al-ism qabl a-zawaaj

mail بريد ba-reed

main رئيسي ra-'ee-see

make يجعل yaj-Aal

man رجل rajol

manage يدير yo-deer; **to manage to do something** ينجح في عمل yan-jaH fee Aamal

manager مدير/مديرة mo-deer (m)/ mode-raa (f)

many كثير ka-theer; **how many?** كم؟ kam?; **how many times?** كم مرة؟ kam mar-ra?

map خريطة kha-ree-Ta **16, 78**

March مارس maa-res, اذار aa-dhaar

marina ميناء لليخوت me-naa' lil-yo-khoot

market سوق sooq **95**

married متزوج motazw-wij

match (for fire) كبريت kab-reet;

(game) مباراة mobaraa

material مادة maa-da

matter: it doesn't matter لا يهم laa ya-homm

mattress مرتبة mar-taba

May مايو maa-yo, أيار a-yaar

maybe ربما rob-bama

me ـني ne; **me too** أنا أيضاً ana ay-Dan

meal وجبة waj-ba

mean يعني yaA-nee; **what does ... mean?** ماذا يعني ...؟ ma-dha yaA-nee ...?

medicine دواء da-waa'

medium متوسط motawas-siT; (meat) نصف سوي neSf sewa

meet يلتقي yal-taqee **70**

meeting اجتماع ig-ti-maaA

member عضو/عضوة AoDoo (m)/ AoD-wah (f)

menu قائمة الطعام qaa-'emat al-Ta-Aaam

message رسالة re-saala

meter عدّاد Aad-daad

metre متر mitr

microwave ميكروووف micro-wave

midday ظهر Zohr

middle وسط wasaT

midnight منتصف الليل mon-taSaf al-layl

might: it might rain ربما rob-bama

mind: I don't mind يمانع yomaa-niA

mine لي lee

mineral water مياه معدنية me-yaah maAda-nay-ya

minute دقيقة daqee-qa; **at the last minute** في اللحظة الأخيرة fee al-laH-Za al-akhee-ra

mirror مرآة mir-'aah

Miss آنسة *aa-nisa*

miss يلحق ب لم *lam yal-Haq be* **34**;
we missed the train لم نلحق
بالقطار *lam nal-Haq bel-qe-Taar*;
there are two … missing …
هناك اثنان من مفقودين *hu-naak ithnaan
min … maf-qoo-deen*

mistake غلطة *ghal-Ta*

mobile (phone) محمول *maH-mool*

modern حديث *Ha-deeth*

moisturizer مرطّب *moraT-Tib*

moment لحظة *laH-Za*

Monday الإثنين *al-ith-nayn*

money مال *maal* **92, 93**

month شهر *shahr*

monument مكان أثري *makaan
atha-ree*

moon قمر *qamar*

more أكثر *akthar*; **more than**
أكثر من *akhtar min*; **much more**
أكثر كثيراً/الأكثركثيراً *akthar kathee-
ran/akhtar beka-theer*; **there's
no more …** … لا يوجد مزيد من … *laa
yoo-jad ma-zeed min …*

morning صباح *Sa-baaH*

Morocco المغرب *al-magh-rib*

mosque مسجد *mas-jid*

mosquito ناموسة *namoo-sa*

most: the most معظم *moA-Zam*;
most people معظم الناس *moA-
Zam al-naas*

mother أم *umm*

motorbike دراجة نارية *dar-raa-ja
naa-ray-ya*

motorway الطريق السريع *al-Ta-reeq
al-sa-reeA*

mountain جبل *jabal*

mouse فأرة *fa-ra*

mouth فم *famm*

movie فيلم *film*

Mr سيد *say-yid*

Mrs سيدة *say-yada*

much كثير *ka-theer*; **how much
is it?, how much does it
cost?** كم سعر هذا؟. *Kam siAr ha-
dha*

mummy (Egyptian) مومياء *mom-
yaa'*

muscle عضلة *AaDala*

museum متحف *mat-Haf*

music موسيقى *moo-see-qa*

must يجب *ya-jib*; **it must be 5
o'clock** لابد أنها الساعة الخامسة الان
*la-bod an-naha al-saa-Aa al-kha-
misa al-aan*; **I must go** يجب ان
أذهب الان *ya-jib an adh-hab al-aan*

my ـي *ee*

N

nail مسمار *mos-maar*

naked عاري *Aaa-ree*

name اسم *ism* **45**

nap غفوة *ghaf-wa*; **to have a nap**
يُقيّل *yoqay-yel*

napkin منديل *man-deel*

national holiday عطلة وطنية *AoT-
la waTanay-ya*

nature طبيعة *Ta-bee-Aa*

near قرب *qorb*

necessary لازم *laa-zim*

neck عنق *Aonoq*

need حاجة *Haa-ja*

neighbour جار *jaar*

neither ولا أنا أيضا *wala ana ay-Dan*

nervous عصبي *AaSa-bee*

never أبدا *abadan*

new جديد *jadeed*

news أخبار *akh-baar*

newspaper جريدة *ja-ree-da*

next بعد baAd
New Year عام جديد Aaam jadeed
nice لطيف lateef
night ليلة lay-la 46
nightclub نادي ليلي naa-dee lay-lee
Nile النيل neel
Nile cruise رحلة نيلية riHla nee-lay-ya
no لا la
nobody لا أحد la aHad
noise ضوضاء Dow-Daa'
non-drinking water ماء غير صالح للشرب maa' ghayr Saa-liH lil-shorb
none لا شيء la-shay'
non-smoker غير مدخّن ghayr modakh-khin
noon ظهر Zohr
north شمال shamaal; **in the north** في الشمال fee al-shamaal; **(to the) north of...** من ناحية الشمال من naa-Hayat al-shamaal min ...
nose أنف anf
not ليس lay-sa
note ملاحظة molaa-HaZa
notebook مفكرة mofak-kira
nothing لا شيء la-shay'
novel رواية rowa-ya
November نوفمبر november, تشرين الثاني tish-reen al-thaa-nee
now الآن al-aan
nowadays في هذه الأيام fee ha-dh-he al-ay-yaam
nowhere لا مكان laa makaan
number عدد Aadad
nurse ممرضة momar-riDa (m)/momar-riDa (f)

O

oasis واحة waa-Ha

obvious واضح waa-DiH
ocean محيط mo-HeeT
o'clock: one o'clock الساعة al-saa-Aa
October أكتوبر oktoober, تشرين الأوّل tish-treen al-aw-wal
of من min
offer عرض AarD
often غالبا ghaa-liban
oil زيت zayt
ointment مرهم mar-ham
OK تمام tamaam
old عمر Aomr; **how old are you?** كم عمرك؟ kam Aom-rak?; **old people** كبار السن ke-baar al-sinn
Oman عمان Ao-maan
on في fee; **it's on at** يعرض في yoA-raD fee
once مرّة واحدة mar-ra waa-Hida
one واحد/واحدة waa-Hid (m)/waa-Hida (f)
only فقط faqaT
open (adj) مفتوح maf-tooH
open (v) يفتح yaf-taH
operate يشغل yoshagh-ghil
operation: to have an operation يعمل عملية yaA-mil Aama-lay-ya
opinion رأي ra'yy; **in my opinion** في رأيي fee ra'y-yee
opportunity فرصة for-Sa
opposite (n) عكس Aaks
opposite (prep) أمام amaam
optician طبيب عيون Tabeeb Aoyoon
or أو aw
orange (adj) برتقالي borto-qaa-lee
orchestra فرقة موسيقية firqa moo-see-qay-ya
order (n) نظام neZaam; **out of**

order لا يعمل laa yaA-mal

order (v) يطلب yaT-lob 56

organic عضوي AoD-wee

organize ينظم yonaZ-Zim

other آخر aa-khar

otherwise خلاف ذلك khilaaf dha-lik

our ـنا na

ours خاصتنا khaaS-Sat-na

outside في الخارج fee al-khaa-rij

oven فرن forn

over: over there هناك hu-naak

overdone مهري mah-ree

**overweight: my luggage is
overweight** حقيبتي زائدة الوزن Ha-
qee-batee zaa-'idat al-wazn

owe مدين madeen 59, 94

own (adj) ـتي tee; **my own car**
سيارتي say-ya-ra-tee

own (v) يملك yam-lok

owner مالك/مالكة maa-lik (m)/maa-
lika (f)

---

pack: to pack one's suitcase
يحزم yaH-zim

packed محزوم maH-zoom

packet ربطة rabTa

painting صورة زيتية Soo-ra zay-
tay-ya

pair زوج zawj; **a pair of pyjamas**
بيجامتين be-jaa-matayn; **a pair of
shorts** شورتين shortayn

palace قصر qaSr

Palestine فلسطين felas-Teen

pants بنطلون banTa-loon

paper ورق waraq; **paper napkin**
فوطة ورق foo-Ta waraq; **paper
tissue** منديل ورق man-deel waraq

parcel طرد Tard

pardon? معذرة! ماذا قلت؟ maA-dhira!
maa-dha qolt?

parents والدان waa-ledaan

park (n) منتزه mon-taza

park (v) يركن السيارة yar-kin al-say-
ya-ra

parking space مكان لركن السيارة
makaan le-rakn al-say-ya-ra

part جزء joz'; **to be a part of** يكون
جزء من yakoon joz' min

party حزب Hizb

pass (n) اشتراك ish-tiraak

pass (v) يمر ya-morr

passenger مسافر mosaa-fir

passport جواز سفر jawaaz safar

past و wa; **a quarter past ten**
العاشرة والربع al-Aaa-shira wa
al-robA

path ممر mamarr

patient (n) مريض/مريضة ma-reeD
(m)/مريضة ma-ree-Da (f)

pay يدفع yad-faA 93, 94

pedestrian مشاه mo-shaa

pee يتبول tabaw-wal

peel قشر qishr

pen قلم qalam

pencil قلم رصاص qalam ro-SaaS

people الناس al-naas

percent بالمئة bel-me-'a

perfect كامل kaa-mil

perfume عطر AeTr

perhaps ربما rob-bama

periods فترات fata-raat

person شخص shakhS

personal stereo كاسيت شخصي
kaset shakh-See

petrol بنزين ban-zeen

petrol station محطة بنزين maHaT-
Tat ban-zeen

phone (n) تليفون tele-foon

phone (v) يتصل ب yat-taSil

phone box كشك تليفون koshk tele-foon **114**

phone call مكالمة تليفونية mokaa-lama tele-foo-nay-ya; **to make a phone call** يعمل مكالمة تليفونية ل yaA-mal mokaa-lama tele-foo-nay-ya le

phonecard بطاقة إتّصال هاتفي be-Ta-qat et-ti-Saal haa-te-fee **114**

phone number رقم تليفون raqam tele-foon

photo صورة Soo-ra **101**; **to take a photo (of)** يأخذ صورة ل ya'-khodh Soo-ra le; **to take someone's photo** يأخذ صورة ل ya'-khodh Soo-ra le

picnic نزهة خلوية noz-ha khalaway-ya

pie فطيرة fatee-ra

piece قطعة qiT-Aa; **a piece of** من قطعة qiT-Aah min; **a piece of fruit** حبة فاكهة Hab-bat faa-kiha

piles أكوام ak-waam

pill حبة Hab-ba

pillow وسادة we-saa-da

pillowcase غطاء وسادة ghe-Taa' we-saa-da

PIN (number) الرقم الشخصي al-raqam al-shakh-See

pink قرنفلي qoron-folee

pity: it's a pity مُحزن moH-sin

place مكان makaan

plan خطة kheT-Ta

plane طائرة Taa-'e-ra

plant نبات nabaat

plaster (cast) لاصق laa-Siq

plastic بلاستيك blastic

plastic bag كيس لبلاستيك kees blastic

plate لوحة/طبق law-Ha/Tabaq

platform رصيف ra-Seef **37**

play (n) مسرحية masra-Hay-ya

play (v) يلعب yal-Aab

please من فضلك min-faD-lak/min-faD-lik (f)

pleased مسرور mas-roor; **pleased to meet you!** انا مسروربلقتك! ana mas-roor be-liqaa-'ak!

pleasure سعادة sa-Aaada

plug فيشة fee-sha

plug in يوصل الفيشة yowaS-Sil al-fee-sha

plumber سبّاك sab-baak

point نقطة noq-Ta

police شرطة shor-Ta

police station مركز شرطة markaz shor-Ta **129**

poor فقير fa-qeer

port ميناء me-naa'

portrait صورة Soo-ra

possible ممكن mom-kin

post بريد ba-reed

postbox صندوق بريد Son-dooq **108**

postcard كارت بريدي kart ba-ree-dee

postcode رمز بريدي ramz ba-ree-dee

poster ملصق mol-Saq

postman ساعي البريد saa-Aee ba-reed

post office مكتب البريد mak-tab al-ba-reed **108**

pound رطل raTl

powder بودرة bod-ra

practical عملي Aama-lee

prefer يفضل yofaD-Dil

pregnant حامل Haa-mil **124**

prepare يعدّ yo-Aedd

present هدية haday-ya

press يضغط yaD-ghaT

pressure ضغط DaghT

previous سابق saa-biq
price سعر siAr
private خاص khaaS
prize جائزة jaa-'iza
probably على الأرجح Ala al-ar-jaH
problem مشكلة mosh-kila
procession موكب mow-kib
product منتج mon-taj
profession مهنة mih-na
programme برنامج barnaa-mij
promise وعد waAd
propose يقترح yaq-tariH
protect يحمي yaH-mee
proud (of) فخور ب fa-khoor be
public جمهور jom-hoor
public holiday عطلة عامة AoT-la
Aaam-ma
pull سحب saHb
purple بنفسجي banaf-sijee
purpose: on purpose عمد Aamd
purse محفظة maH-faZa
push دفع dafA
put يضع yaDaA
put up with يتحمّل yataHam-mal
Pyramid هرم haram

Q

Qatar قطر qaTar
quality نوعية now-Aay-ya
quarter ربع robA; **a quarter of
an hour** ربع ساعة robA saa-Aa;
a quarter to ten العاشرة إلا ربع
al-Aaa-shira il-la robA
quay رصيف الميناء ra-Seef al-mee-
naa'
question سؤال so-'aal
queue (n) طابور Taa-boor
queue (v) يقف في الطابور yaqif fee
al-Taa-boor

quick سريع sa-reeA
quickly سريعا sa-ree-Aan
quiet هادئ haa-de'
quite تماماً tamaa-man

R

racist عنصري Aon-Soree
racket مضرب maD-rab
radiator ردياتير rad-yaa-ter
radio راديو rad-yoo
radio station محطة راديو maHaT-
Tat rad-yoo
rain مطر maTar
rain: (v) **it's raining** تمطر tom-Tir
raincoat عطف واق من المطر miA-Taf
waa-qee min al-maTar
random: at random عشوائي
Aash-waa-'ee
rape إغتصاب egh-tiSaab
rare نادر naa-dir; (meat) نيء nay'
rarely نادرا naa-diran
rather بالأحرى bel-aHraa
raw خام khaam
razor ماكينة حلاقة makee-nat
He-laa-qa
razor blade شفرة حلاقة shaf-rat
He-laa-qa
reach يصل ya-Sil
read يقرأ yaq-ra'
ready مستعد mos-taAed
reasonable معقول maA-qool
receipt إيصال ee-Saal 94, 125
receive يستلم yas-talim
reception استقبال is-tiq-baal; **at
reception** بالاستقبال bel-is-tiq-
baal 49
receptionist موظف استقبال mo-
waZ-Zaf is-tiq-baal
recipe وصفة waS-fa

recognize يميّز yomay-yez

recommend يوصي yo-See 47, 54

red أحمر aH-mar

red light ضوء أحمر Doo' aH-mar

red wine خمر أحمر khamr aH-mar

reduce يقلل yokhaf-fiD

reduction تخفيض takh-feeD

refrigerator ثلاجة thal-laa-ja

refund (n) استرداد الثمن is-tir-daad al-thaman; to get a refund يسترد الثمن yas-taridd al-thaman

refund (v) يسترد الثمن yas-taridd al-thaman

refuse قمامة qe-maa-ma

registered مسجّل mosaj-jal

registration number رقم التسجيل raqam al-tas-jeel

remember يتذكر yatazak-kar

remind يذكر yodhak-kir

remove يزيل yo-zeel

rent (n) إيجار ee-jaar

rent (v) يستأجر yasta'-jir 50

rental إيجار ee-jaar

reopen يفتح ثانية yaf-taH thaa-neyatan

repair إصلاح iS-laaH 40; to get something repaired يصلّح yoSal-liH

repeat تكرار tik-raar 13

reserve احتياطي iHte-yaa-Tee 46, 55

reserved محجوز maH-jooz

rest: (n) the rest بقية baqay-ya

rest (v) يستريح yasta-reeH

restaurant مطعم maT-Aam

return عودة Aow-da

return ticket تذكرة عودة tadh-kara Aow-da

rheumatism روماتيزم romaa-tizm

rib ضلع DilA

right (n) حق Haqq; to have the right to ... يكون له الحق في ... yakoon la-hu al-Haqq fee ...; to the right (of) إلي ناحية اليمين من ila naa-Heyat al-ya-meen min

right (adj) صواب Sawaab

right: (adv) right away حالاً Haa-lan; right beside بجانب be-jaa-nib

ripe يانع yaa-niA

rip-off نصب naSb

risk خطر khaTar

river نهر nahr

road طريق Ta-reeq

road sign إشارة طريق eshaa-rat Ta-reeq

rock صخرة Sakh-ra

room غرفة ghor-fa 46, 47, 48

round مستدير mosta-deer

roundabout دوّار daw-waar

rubbish زبالة ze-baala; to take the rubbish out يلقي الزبالة yol-qee al-ze-baala ba-Aee-dan بعيداً

rug سجّادة sij-jaa-da

ruins أطلال aT-laal; in ruins مُدمَّر modam-mar

run out: to have run out of petrol ينفذ ما لديه من وقود yan-fadh maa laday-he min wa-qood 40

S

sad حزين Ha-zeen

safe آمن aa-min

safety أمان amaan

safety belt حزام أمان he-zaam amaan

sail شراع she-raaA

sailing الإبحار بالمراكب الشراعية aleb-Haar bil-maraa-kib al-she-raa-Aay-ya; **to go sailing** يبحر yob-Hir

sale: for sale للبيع lil-beeA

sales تخفيضات الاسعار takhfee-Daat al-as-Aaar

salt ملح malH

salted يملح yomal-liH

salty مالح maa-liH

same نفس nafs 59

sand رمل raml

sandals صندل Sun-dal

Saturday السبت al-sabt

saucepan حلّة طبيخ Hal-lat Ta-beekh

Saudi Arabia العربية السعودية al-mam-laka al-Aara-bay-ya al-soAoo-day-ya

save باستثناء bes-tith-naa'

say يقول yaqool; **how do you say ... in Arabic?** باللغة ... كيف تقول العربية؟ Keyfa taqool ... bel-logha al-Aara-bay-ya?

scared: to be scared (of) خائف khaa-'if

scenery مشهد mash-Had

scissors مقص me-qaSS

scoop (of ice cream) بولة boo-la

scuba diving جهاز الغوص je-haaz

sea بحر baHr

seafood فواكه البحر fawaa-kih al-baHr

seasick: to be seasick دوار البحر dow-waar al-baHr

seaside: at the seaside جانب البحر jaa-nib al-baHr

seaside resort منتجع بجانب البحر mon-tajaA be-jaa-nib al-baHr

season فصل faSl

seat مقعد miq-Aad 32

sea view منظر مطلّ علي البحر man-

Zar mo-Till Aala al-baHr

second ثاني thaa-nee

secondary school مدرسة ثانوية mad-rasa thaa-na-way-ya

second-hand مستعمل mos-taA-mal

secure مأمون ma'-moon

security أمن amn

see يري yara; **see you later!** أراك لاحقاً araa-ka laa-Hiqan; **see you soon!** أراك قريباً araa-ka qa-reeban!; **see you tomorrow!** أراك غداً araa-ka ghadan!

seem يبدو yab-do; **it seems that ...** يبدو أن... yab-do an-na ...

seldom نادراً naa-diran

sell يبيع ya-beeA

send يرسل yor-sil

sender مُرسِل/مُرسلة mor-sil (m)/ mor-sila (f)

sense حس Hiss

sensitive حساس Has-saas

sentence جملة jom-la

separate منفصل mon-faSil

separately على حدة Aala Hida

September سبتمبر seb-tam-ber, أيلول ay-lool

serious جدي jid-dee

several عدة Aed-da

shade ظل Zill; **in the shade** في الظل fee al-Zill

shame عار Aaar

shampoo شامبو sham-boo

shape شكل shakl

share يشارك yo-shaa-rik

shave حلاقة He-laa-qa

shaving cream كريم حلاقة kream He-laa-qa

shaving foam رغوة حلاقة ragh-wat He-laa-qa

she هي he-ya

sheet ورق waraq
shirt قميص qa-meeS
shock صدمة Sad-ma
shocking فظيع fa-ZeeA
shoes أحذية aH-dhe-ya
shop متجر mat-jar
shop assistant مساعد مبيعات mosaa-Aed ma-bee-Aaat
shopkeeper صاحب المحل Saa-Hib al-maHal
shopping تسوق tasow-woq; **to do some/the shopping** يتسوق yatasow-waq
shopping centre مركز تسوق markaz tasow-woq
short محتاج moH-taaj; **I'm two ... short** أنا محتاج اثنين ... ana moH-taaj ...
short cut طريق مختصر Ta-reeq mokh-taSar
shorts شورت short
short-sleeved نصف كم neSf komm
shoulder كتف ketf
show (n) عرض AarD
show (v) يعرض yaA-riD
shower دش dosh
shower gel جل الإستحمام jel al-is-tiH-maam
shut يغلق yogh-liq
shuttle مكوك ma-kook
shy خجلان khaj-laan (m)/khaj-laa-na (f)
sick: to feel sick غثيان ghath-yaan
side جانب jaa-nib
sign (n) علامة Aalaa-ma
sign (v) يوقع yo-waq-qiA
signal إشارة ishaa-ra
silent صامت Saa-mit
silver فضة faD-Da

since منذ mondh
sing يغني yoghan-nee
singer مغني/مغنية moghan-nee (m)/moghan-nay-ya (f)
single (person) أعزب aA-zab
single (ticket) ذهاب dhe-haab
sister أخت okht
sit down يجلس yaj-lis
size مقاس ma-qaas
ski زلاجة zal-laa-ja
skin جلد jild
skirt جيبة jee-ba
sky سماء samaa'
skyscraper ناطحة سحاب naa-TiHat sa-Haab
sleep (n) نوم nowm
sleep (v) ينام ya-naam; **to sleep with** ينام مع ya-naam maAa
sleeping bag كيس للنوم kees lil-nowm
sleeping pill حبوب مساعدة للنوم Ho-boob mosaa-Aeda lil-nowm
sleepy: to be sleepy نعسان naA-saan
sleeve كم komm
slice شريحة sha-ree-Ha
sliced مقطّع شرائح moqaT-TaA sha-raa-'iH
slide مجموعة صور maj-moo-Aat So-war
slow بطئ ba-Tee'
slowly ببطء be-boT'
small صغير Sa-gheer
smell (n) رائحة raa-'iHa
smell (v) يشم رائحة yashomm raa-'iHa; **to smell good/bad** له رائحة ذكية/كريهة la-hu raa-'iHa za-kay-ya/ka-ree-ha
smoke دخان dokh-khaan
smoker مدخن/مدخنة modakh-khin

(m)/modakh-khina (f)

snack وجبة خفيفة waj-ba khafee-fa

snow (n) ثلج thalj

snow (v) تمطر ثلج tom-Tir thalj

so لذا le-dha; **so that** لكي le-kay

soap صابون Sa-boon

soccer كرة قدم korat qadam

socks جورب jow-rab

some بعض baAD; **some people** بعض الناس baAD al-naas

somebody, someone شخص ما shakh-Son ma

something شيئ shay'; **something else** شيئ اخر shay' aa-khar

sometimes أحيانا aH-yaa-nan

somewhere في مكان ما fee makaan ma; **somewhere else** في مكان اخر fee makaan aa-khar

son إبن ibn

song أغنية ogh-nay-ya

soon قريبا qa-ree-ban

sore: to have a sore throat لديه إلتهاب في الحلق laday-he il-tihaab fee al-Halq; **to have a sore head** لديه الالم في الرأس laday-he aa-laam fee al-ra's

sorry آسف/آسفة aa-sef (m)/aa-sefa (f)

south جنوب ja-noob; **in the south** في الجنوب fee al-ja-noob; **(to the) south of** في الناحية الجنوبية من fee al-naa-Hiya al-jano-bay-ya

souvenir تذكار tidh-kaar

spare زائد zaa-'id

spare part قطع غيار qeTaA ghe-yaar

spare tyre اطار احتياطي iTaar iHte-yaa-Tee

spare wheel عجلة احتياطية Aajalat iHte-yaa-Tay-ya

spark plug مشعل mish-Aal

speak يتكلم yatakal-lam **11, 13, 14, 115, 129**

special خاص khaaS

speciality اختصاص ikhti-SaaS

speed سرعة sor-Aa

spell يتهجئ yatahaj-ja'

spend ينفق yon-fiq

Sphinx أبو الهول abu al-hool

spice تابل taa-bil

spicy حار Haar

spider عنكبوت Aanka-boot

splinter شظية shaZ-ya

split up ينفصل yan-faSil

spoil يفسد yaf-sad

sponge إسفنجة is-fin-ja

spoon ملعقة mal-Aaqa

sport رياضة re-yaa-Da

sports ground أماكن لممارسة الرياضة amaa-kin le-momaa-rasat al-re-yaa-Da

sporty رياضي re-raa-Dee

spot موضع mow-DiA

sprain (v) جزعة jaz-Aa

spring نبع ماء nabA maa'

square مربع morab-baA

stadium استاد is-taad

stain بقعة boq-Aa

stairs سلالم sa-laa-lim

stamp طابع Taa-biA **108**

start بداية be-daa-ya

state دولة dow-la

statement بيان bayaan

station محطة maHaT-Ta

stay (n) بقاء ba-qaa'

stay (v) يبقى yab-qa; **to stay in touch** يبقى على اتصال مع yab-qa Aala it-ti-Saal maAa

steal يسرق yas-riq **129**

step خطوة khaT-wa

still بعد baAd

still water ماء غير فوار maa' ghayr fow-waar

sting (n) قرصة qar-Sa

sting (v) يقرص yaq-roS; **to get stung by** يصاب بقرصة من yo-Saab be-qa-Sa min

stock: out of stock مخزون makh-zoon

stomach معدة meA-da

stone حجارة He-jaa-ra

stop (n) توقف tawaq-quf

stop (v) يتوقف yatawaq-qaf

storm عاصفة Aaa-Sefa

straight ahead, straight on طوالي Tow-waa-lee

strange غريب gha-reeb

street شارع shaa-riA

strong قوي qa-wee

stuck ملتصق mol-taSiq

student طالب/طالبة Taa-lib (m)/Taa-liba (f) 32

studies دراسات deraa-saat

study دراسة de-raa-sa

style أسلوب os-loob

subtitled به شريط ترجمة be-he sha-reeT tar-jama

suburb ضاحية Daa-Hiya

suffer يعاني yoAaa-nee

suggest يقترح yaq-tariH

suit: does that suit you? هل هذا يناسبك؟ hal ha-dha yonaa-sibak?

suitcase حقيبة Ha-qee-ba 34

summer فصل الصيف faSl al-Sayf

summit قمة qim-ma

sun شمس shams

sunbathe حمّام شمس Ham-maam shams

sunburnt: to get sunburnt لفحة شمس laf-Hit shams

sun cream كريم حماية من اشعة الشمس kream He-maa-ya min ashiA-Aat al-shams

Sunday يوم الأحد yawm al-aHad

sunglasses نظارة شمس naZ-Zaa-ra shams

sunhat طاقية شمس Taa-qay-ya shams

sunrise شروق sho-rooq

sunset غروب gho-roob

sunstroke ضربة شمس Dar-bat shams; **to get sunstroke** يصاب بضربة شمس yo-Saab be-Dar-bat shams

supermarket مركز تسوق كبير mar-kaz tasow-woq ka-beer 92

supplement ملحق mol-Haq

sure متأكد mota'ak-kid

surf ركوب الأمواج ro-koob al-am-waaj

surfboard لوح ركوب الأمواج lowH ro-koob al-am-waaj

surfing ركوب الامواج ro-koob al-am-waaj; **to go surfing** يركب الأمواج ya-kab al-am-waaj

surname إسم العائلة ism al-Aaa-'ila

surprise (n) مفاجأة mofaa-ja'a

surprise (v) يفاجئ yofaa-ji'

sweat عرق Aaraq

sweater سويتر so-weater

sweet (n) حلوى Hal-wa

sweet (adj) حلو Helo

swim: (n) to go for a swim العوم al-Aowm

swim (v) يعوم ya-Aoom

swimming سباحة se-baa-Ha

swimming pool حمّام سباحة Ham-maam se-baa-Ha

swimsuit ملابس سباحة malaa-bis se-baa-Ha

switch off يغلق yogh-liq

switch on يفتح yaf-taH
switchboard operator عامل السويتش Aaa-mil al-switch
swollen وارم waa-rim
Syria سوريا soo-re-ya
syrup شراب sha-raab

T

table طاولة Tow-la **55**
tablespoon ملعقة طعام mal-Aaqat Ta-Aaam
tablet قرص qorS
take يأخذ ya'-khodh
take off (plane) تقلع toq-leA
talk محادثة moHaa-datha
tall طويل Ta-weel
tampon فوطة صحية نسائية foo-Ta SeH-Hay-ya
tan تلوين الجلد tal-ween al-jild
tanned ملون mo-low-wan
tap حنفية Hanafay-ya
taste ذوق dhowq
tax ضريبة Da-ree-ba
tax-free معفي من الضرائب maA-fee min al-Daraa-'ib
taxi تاكسي tak-see **41**
taxi driver سائق تاكسي saa-'iq tak-see
team فريق fareeq
teaspoon ملعقة شاي mal-Aaqat shaay
teenager مراهق/مراهقة moraa-hiq/moraa-hiqa
telephone (n) تليفون tele-foon
telephone (v) يتصل بالتليفون yat-taSil bil-tele-foon
television تلفزيون fele-vez-yoon
tell يخبر yokh-bir
temperature حرارة Ha-raa-ra; **to**

take one's temperature يقيس الحرارة ya-qees al-Ha-raa-ra
temporary مؤقت mo'aq-qat
tennis لعبة التنس loA-bat al-tenis
tennis court ملعب التنس mal-Aab al-tenis
tennis shoe حذاء التنس Hi-dhaa' al-tenis
tent خيمة khay-ma
tent peg وتد الخيمة watad al-khay-ma
terminal محطة maHaT-Ta
terrace شرفة shor-fa
terrible رهيب ra-heeb
thank شكر shokr; **thank you** شكرا shok-ran; **thank you very much** شكرا جزيلا shok-ran ja-zee-lan
thanks شكرا shok-ran; **thanks to** بفضل be-faDl
that ذاك dha-ka; **that one** ذاك ال dha-ka
the الـ al-
theatre مسرح mas-raH
theft سرقة sariqa
their ـهم hom
theirs خاصتهم khaaS-Sat-hom
them هم hom
then بعد ذلك baAd dha-lik
there هناك hu-naak
therefore لذلك le-dha-lik
thermometer ميزان حرارة me-zaan al-Ha-raa-ra
these هؤلاء ha-olaa'
they هم hom
thief لصّ/الصّة liSS/liS-Sa
thigh فخذ fakhdh
thin رقيق ra-qeeq
thing شيء shay'
think يفكر yofak-kir
thirst عطش AaTash

thirsty: to be thirsty عطشان
AaT-shaan

this هذا ha-dha; **this one** هذا
ha-dha; **this evening** المساء هذا
ha-dha al-masaa'; **this is** هو هذا
ha-dha hu-wa

those هؤلاء ha-olaa'; **those ones**
h, ha-olaa'

throat حلق Halq

throw يرمي yar-mee

throw out يلقي بعيداً yol-qee
baAee-dan

Thursday يوم الخميس yawm al-kha-
mees

ticket تذكرة tadh-kara **32, 72, 73**

ticket office مكتب التذاكر mak-tab
al-tadhaa-kir

tidy مرتب morat-tab

tight ضيق Day-yiq

time وقت waqt; **what time is it?**
kam al-saa-Aa al-
aan?; **from time to time** من حين
min Heen ila aa-khar; **on** الي اخر
time في الوقت المحدد fee al-waqt al-
moHad-dad; **three/four times**
tha-laath/arbaA ثلاث/أربع مرات
mar-raat

time difference فرق التوقيت farq
tow-qeet

timetable جدول المواعيد jad-wal
al-mawaa-Aeed **32**

tinfoil ورق الومنيوم waraq alamon-
yom

tip بقشيش baq-sheesh

tired تعبان taA-baan

tobacco تبغ tabgh

today اليوم al-yawm

together معاً maAan

toilet حمّام Ham-maam **11, 54**

toilet paper ورق تواليت waraq

towa-lit

toiletries ادوات الحمّام والزينة adwaat
al-Ham-maam wa al-zee-na

tomb مقبرة maq-bara

tomorrow غدا ghadan

tongue لسان lisaan

tonight هذا المساء ha-dha al-masaa'

too للغاية lil-ghaa-ya; **too bad**
سيء للغاية say-yi' lil-ghaa-ya; **too**
many كثير للغاية ka-theer lil-ghaa-
ya; **too much** كثير للغاية ka-theer
lil-ghaa-ya

tooth سنّة sin-na

toothbrush فرشاة أسنان for-shat
as-naan

toothpaste معجون أسنان maA-joon
as-naan

top قمة qim-ma; **at the top** علي
قمة Aala al-qim-ma

torch كشّاف kash-shaaf

touch لمسة lam-sa

tourist سائح/سائحة saa-'iH (m)/
saa-'iHa (f)

tourist information centre
مكتب السياحة mak-tab al-se-yaa-
Ha **78**

tourist trap حنطور سياحي Han-
Toor

towards نحو naHo

towel فوطة foo-Ta

town مدينة madee-na

toy لعبة loA-ba

traditional تقليدي taq-lee-dee

traffic حركة مرور Haraka al-mo-
roor

train قطار qe-Taar **37**; **to take the**
train to Aswan يستقل القطارالي
yas-taqil al-qe-Taar ila أسوان

train station محطة قطار maHaT-
Tat qe-Taar

translate يترجم yotar-jim
travel agency وكيل سياحي wakeel se-yaa-Hee
travel سفر safar
traveller's cheque شبكات سياحية she-kat se-ya-Hay-a
trip رحلة riHla
trousers بنطلون banta-loon
true صحيح Sa-HeeH
try يحاول yo-Haa-wel; **to try to do something** يحاول ان يقوم بـ yo-Haa-wil an ya-qoom be
try on يقيس ya-qees
Tuesday يوم الثلاثاء yawm al-thola-thaa'
Tunisia تونس too-nis
turn: (n) **it's your turn** دور door
turn (v) يلف ya-liff
twice مرتين mar-ratayn
type (n) طباعة Te-baa-Aa
type (v) يطبع yaT-baA
typical نموذجي namoo-zaj
tyre إطار e-Taar

U

umbrella شمسية sham-say-ya
uncle عم Aamm
uncomfortable غير مرتاح ghayr mer-taaH
under تحت taHt
underground مترو الانفاق metro al-an-faaq
underneath تحت taHt
understand يفهم yaf-ham **13**, **14**
underwear ملابس داخلية malaa-bis daa-khe-lay-ya
United Arab Emirates الإمارات العربية المتحدة al-imaa-raat al-Aara-bay-ya al-mot-taHida

United Kingdom المملكة المتحدة al-mam-laka al-mot-taHida
until حتى Hat-ta
upstairs الدور الأعلى al-door al-arDee
urgent ملح mo-liH
us نا na
use يستخدم yastakh-dim; **to be used for** يستخدم لـ yostakh-dam le; **I'm used to it** انا معتاد علي ana moA-taad Aala
useful مفيد mofeed
useless غير مفيد ghayr mofeed
usually عادة Aaa-datan

V

vaccinated محصّن ضد moHaS-San Did
valid (for) صالح لـ Saa-liH le
valid صالح Saa-liH
valley واد waa-dee
VAT ضريبة المبيعات Da-ree-bat al-mabee-Aaat
vegetarian نباتي nabaa-tee
very جداً jid-dan
view منظر man-Zar
villa فيلا vil-la
village قرية qar-ya
visa تأشيرة ta'-shee-ra
visit (n) زيارة ze-yaa-ra
visit (v) يزور yazoor
vomit قيء qee'

W

waist وسط wasaT
wait ينتظر yan-taZir; **to wait for somebody/something** ينتظر شخصشيء/ينتظر yan-taZir shakhS/ shay'

waiter نادل *naa-dil*

waitress نادلة *naa-dila*

wake up يستيقظ *yastay-qiZ*

walk: (n) **to go for a walk** جولة قصيرة *jow-la qa-See-ra*

walk (v) يمشي *yam-shee*

walking: to go walking ماشيا *maa-she-yan*

wallet محفظة *maH-faZa*

want يريد *yo-reed*; **to want to do something** يريد القيام بـ *yo-reed al-qe-yaam be*

warm دافئ *daa-fi'*

warn يحذر *yoHadh-dhir*

wash: (n) **to have a wash** يغتسل *yagh-tasil*

wash يغسل *yagh-sil*; **to wash one's hair** يغسل شعره *yagh-sil shaA-roh*

washbasin حوض *howD*

washing: to do the washing غسيل الملابس *gha-seel al-malaa-bis*

washing machine غسّالة الملابس *ghas-saa-lat al-malaa-bis*

washing powder مسحوق الغسيل *mas-Hooq al-gha-seel*

washing-up liquid سائل غسيل الاطباق *saa-'il gha-seel al-aT-baaq*

wasp دبور *dab-boor*

waste نفاية *nifaa-ya*

watch (n) مشاهدة *moshaa-hada*

watch (v) يشاهد *yoshaa-hid*; **watch out!** خلّي بالك! *Khal-lee baa-lak!*

water ماء *maa'*

water heater سخّان ماء *sakh-khaan maa'*

waterpipe شيشة *sheesha*

waterproof ضد الماء *Did al-maa'*

waterskiing التزحلق على الماء *al-*

wave موجة *moo-ja*

way طريق *Ta-reeq*

way in الطريق الى الداخل *al-Ta-reeq ila al-daa-khil*

way out الطريق الي الخارج *al-Ta-reeq ila al-khaa-rij*

we نحن *naH-nu*

weak ضعيف *Da-Aeef*

wear يلبس *yal-bis*

weather طقس *Taqs*; **the weather's bad** الطقس سيء *al-Taqs say-yi'*

weather forecast توقعات الارصاد *ta-waq-qoAaat al-ar-Saad 29*

website موقع علي الانترنت *mow-qiA Aala al-internet*

Wednesday يوم الأربعاء *yawm al-ar-beAaa'*

week أسبوع *os-booA*

weekend نهاية أسبوع *ne-haa-yat al-os-booA*

welcome مرحبا *mar-Haba*; **you're welcome** اهلا بك! *ahlan beka!*

well بخير *be-kheir*; **I'm very well** انا بخير *ana be-kheir*; **well done** (meat) مطهو جيدا *maT-hoo jay-yidan*

well-known معروف *maA-roof*

west غرب *gharb*; **in the west** في الغرب *fee al-gharb*; **(to the) west of** بإتجاه ناحية الغرب *be-ti-jaah naa-Heyat al-gharb*

wet مبلل *mobal-lal*

what ماذا *ma-dha*; **what do you want?** ماذا تريد؟ *ma-dha to-reed?*

wheel عجلة *Aajala*

wheelchair كرسي متحرك *kor-see mota-Har-rik*

when عندما *Aen-dama*

where أين *ayna*; **where is/are?** أين *ayna*; **where are you from?** من أين أنت؟ *min ayna an-ta?*; **where are you going?** إلي أين تذهب؟ *ila ayna tadh-hab?*

which الذي *al-la-dhee*

while بينما *bay-nama*

white أبيض *ab-yaD*

who? من؟ *man?*; **who's calling?** من المتحدّث؟ *man al-motaHad-dith?*

whole كل *koll*; **the whole cake** كل الكعكة *koll al-kaA-ka*

whose لمن *li-man?*

why لماذا ؟ *li-ma-dha?*

wide عريض *Aa-reeD*

wife زوجة *zaw-ja*

wild متوحّش *motawaH-Hish*

wind ريح *reeH*

window نافذة *nee-fidha*

wine خمر *khamr*

winter شتاء *she-taa'*

with مع *maAa*

withdraw يسحب *yas-Hib*

without دون *doo-na*

woman إمرأة *im-ra'a*

wonderful رائع *raa-'iA*

wood خشب *khashab*

wool صوف *Soof*

work (n) عمل *Aamal*; **work of art** عمل فني *Aamal fan-nee*

work (v) يعمل *yaA-mal*

works أعمال *aA-maal*

world عالم *Aaa-lam*

worse أسوء *as-wa'*; **to get worse** يصير الي الأسوء *ya-Seer ila al-as-wa'*; **it's worse than** إنه أسوء من *in-nahu as-wa' min*

worth: to be worth قيمة *qee-ma*

wound جرح *jarH*

wrist معصم *miA-Sam*

write يكتب *yak-tob* 14, 17, 94

wrong خطأ *khaTa'*

XYZ

X-rays أشعة اكس *ashiA-Aat X*

year سَنة *sana*

yellow أصفر *aS-far*

Yemen اليمن *al-yaman*

yes نعم *naAam*

yesterday بالأمس *bil-ams*

you أنت *an-ta*

young شاب/شابة *shaab* (m)/*shaab-ba* (f)

your ــك *ka*

yours خاصتك *khaaS-Satak*

zero صفر *Sifr*

zoo حديقة حيوان *Ha-dee-qat haya-waan*

zoom (lens) تكبير *tak-beer*

GRAMMAR

Articles

The **indefinite article** (a/an in English) does not exist in Arabic. A countable noun usually takes the singular form as long as it does not have a dual or plural suffix:

a hotel فندق fon-doq
a ticket تذكرة tadh-kara

The **definite article** (the in English), which stands apart from the noun, is distinguished in Arabic by the prefix الـ (pronounced and transcribed as al). This prefix is used for nouns of any gender or number and is also attached to any adjectives modifying the noun. The **al-** prefix is integrated into words, unlike in English where the stands apart:

the Arabic language	اللغة العربية	al-logha **al**-Aara-bay-ya
the young girls	الفتيات الصغيرات	al-fatayaat **al**-Saghee-raat
the phone book	دليل التليفون	da-leel **al**-tele-foon

Nouns

Nouns in Arabic are either masculine or feminine. Most feminine nouns end in the sound ة (pronounced a). The majority of masculine nouns may be made feminine by adding the suffix ة.

	masculine singular		feminine singular
teacher	مُعلّم	moAal-lim	مُعلّمة moAal-lima
student	طالب	Taa-lib	طالبة Taa-liba
friend	صَديق	Sa-deeq	صَديقة Sa-dee-qa

The a suffix is the marker for the feminine gender form of a noun ending with a ة. This ة is pronounced as ت t only when the noun is followed by another word, typically as in the case of IDaafa (genitive) or by a predicate. For example:

جاءت المعلمة jaa-'at al-moAal-lima (the teacher came)
هذه معلمة العلوم ha-dhe-he muAal-limat al-Aoloom (this is the science teacher)

There are three forms of nouns in Arabic: singular, dual and plural. The dual form applies to the 2nd and 3rd persons and refers to two of anything (roughly the equivalent of saying "you two" or "those two"), so the dual refers to two and the plural to more than two. Forming dual nouns depends on the gender and the case of the noun in a sentence or phrase. To change a masculine singular noun in the nominative case into the dual form, you simply add the suffix ان *aan*. If the nouns are in the accusative, dative or genitive cases, you add the suffix ين *ayn*. A feminine singular noun can be changed into the dual form by adding the suffix تان *taan* in the nominative, and تين *tayn* in the accusative, dative and genitive cases:

masculine

(sing.) a man رجل *rajol*
(dual/nom.) two men رجلان *rajolaan*
(dual/acc., dat., gen.) two men رجلين *rajolayn*

feminine

(sing.) a word كلمة *kalmia*
(dual/nom.) two words كلمتان *kalimataan*
(dual/acc., dat., gen.) two words كلمتين *kalima-tayn*

Plural nouns in Arabic fall into three groups: masculine, feminine and irregular.

درّاجة *dar-ra-ja* (bicycle) → درّاجات *dar-ra-jaat* (bicycles), eg:
هل يوجد مكان لترك الدراجات؟ *hal yoo-jad makaan li-tark al-dar-ra-jaat?*
Do you have somewhere we could leave our bikes?

For the masculine plural form, you add either the suffix ون (*oon*) or the suffix ين (*een*), depending on the position of the noun in the sentence or phrase:

المرشد *al-mor-shid* (guide) → المرشدون *al-mor-shidoon* (guides) in the nominative

المرشد *mor-shid* (guide) → المرشدين *mor-shideen* in the accusative and genitive
حضر المرشدون *HaDara al-mor-shidoon* (the guides arrived)
هل تفتح البنوك أيام السبت؟ *hal taf-taH al-bonook ay-yaam al-sabt?* do banks open on Saturdays?

There is no particular rule for changing single nouns into irregular plural nouns. In most cases, nouns have to be learnt by heart, and they follow certain forms that a non-native speaker will not find easy to remember. Examples of these forms are:

صورة *Soo-ra* (picture)	→	صور *So-war* (pictures)
طالب *Taa-lib* (student)	→	طلبة *Talaba* (students)
تذكرة *tadh-kara* (ticket)	→	تذاكر *tadhaa-kir* (tickets)
لعبة *loA-ba* (game)	→	الألعاب *al-Aaab* (games)

Adjectives

Adjectives come after the noun they describe and agree with it in gender and number. However, in the case of irregular and inanimate nouns, although they are not suffixed by *oon* or *een*, the adjective may still take these endings or the singular form may be used. An adjective applied to a feminine noun will take the suffix ة (pronounced and transcribed *a*).

a small door (masculine) باب صغير *bab Sa-gheer*

two small doors بابين صغيرين / بابان صغيران *ba-bayn Saghee-rayn / ba-baan Saghee-raan*

small doors أبواب صغيرة *ab-waab Saghee-ra*

a new car (feminine) سيارة جديدة *say-ya-ra ja-dee-da*

two new cars سيارتين جديدتين / سيارتان جديدتان *say-ya-ratayn jadee-datayn / say-ya-rataan jadee-dataan*

new cars سيارات جديدات *say-ya-raat jade-daat*

Comparative and superlative adjectives have the same form in Arabic, irrespective of gender. To form them, you must identify the root of the word (the basic form) then add *a* before the root and *a* before the last consonant. In the comparative form, after forming the adjective, you need to follow it with the preposition *min*. In the superlative, you precede the adjective with the definite article *al*:

tall طويل *Ta-weel*

→ the root is ط و ل *Twl*

→ the comparative (taller) will be أطول *aT-wal*

Samy is taller than Hany سامي أطول من هاني *Samy aT-wal min Hany*

the superlative (tallest) will be الأطول *al-aT-wal*

Ahmad is the tallest student in the class أحمد أطول تلميذ في الفصل *AHmad aT-wal til-meedh fee al-faSl*

Adverbs

Adverbs have no specific form in Arabic (unlike in English, where they are often formed by adding -ly to the corresponding adjective, eg slow → slowly). They must simply be learnt as individual items of vocabulary.

Pronouns

There are three types of pronouns: personal pronouns, object pronouns and demonstrative pronouns.

Personal pronouns have 12 forms. The 2nd person (you) and 3rd person (he/she/it) forms both have a separate masculine and feminine form. The 2nd and 3rd persons also have a special form which exists in Arabic called the **dual** form, which refers to two of anything (roughly the equivalent of saying "you two" or "those two"), so the dual refers to two and the plural to more than two.

Personal (subject) pronouns

		dual form
I	أنا an-a	
you (m sing.)	أنت an-ta	
you (f sing.)	أنت an-te	
he	هو hu-wa	
she	هي he-ya	
we	نحن naH-no	
you (m pl.)	أنتم an-tom	أنتما an-toma
you (f pl.)	أنتنّ an-ton-na	أنتما an-toma
they (m)	هم hom	هما hu-ma
they (f)	هن hun-na	هما hu-ma

Object pronouns take the form of suffixes which are affixed to verbs to denote the direct object.

		dual form
me	ي -ee	
you (m sing.)	ك -k	
you (f sing.)	كي -kee	
him	ـه -h	
her	ها -ha	
us	نا -na	
you (m pl.)	كم -kom	كما -koma
you (f pl.)	كنّ -kon-na	كما -koma
them (m)	هم -hom	هما -homa
them (f)	هنّ -hun-na	هما -homa

There are three **demonstrative pronouns** in the Arabic language, **this, that** and **these.**

this (m)	هذا *ha-dha*
this (f)	هذه *ha-dh-he*
that (m)	ذاك *dha-ka*
that (f)	تلك *til-ka*
these (dual m)	هذان *ha-dhaan*
these (pl. dual f)	هاتان *ha-taan*
these/those (pl. m/f)	هؤلاء *ha-olaa'*

book كتاب *ketaab*	
my book كتابي *ketaa-bee*	
our book كتابنا *ketaa-bana*	
your book كتابك *ketaa-bak*	
your book (dual m/f) كتابكما *ketaa-bakoma*	
your book (pl. m) كتابكم *ketaa-bakom*	
your book (pl. f) كتابكن *ketaa-bakon-na*	
his book كتابه *ketaa-baho*	
her book كتابها *ketaa-baha*	
their book (dual m/f) كتابهما *ketaa-bahoma*	
their book (pl. m) كتابهم *ketaa-bahom*	
their book (pl. f) كتابهن *ketaa-bahon-na*	

To form an object pronoun, you just attach the appropriate suffix to the noun. Unlike in English, with Arabic object pronouns you will need to repeat the noun in the second part of a sentence (the noun *ketaab* is mentioned twice). Please note letters added between the noun and the suffixes are not part of the original word and do not appear in the Arabic script. They just stand for the particular sound required to vowel the noun according to its position in a sentence. (See for example *a* in *ketaa-bak*).

this is your book and this mine (first/sing.) هذا كتابك وهذا كتابي
ha-dha ketaa-bak wa ha-dha ketaa-bee
this is my book and that is yours (second/sing.) هذا كتابي وهذا كتابك
ha-dha ketaa-bee wa ha-dha ketaa-bak
this is your book and this hers (third/sing. f) هذا كتابك وهذا كتابها
ha-dha ketaa-bak wa hadha ketaa-baha
this is your book and this his (third/sing. m) هذا كتابك وهذا كتابه
ha-dha ketaa-bak wa ha-dha ketaa-boh

this is your book and this theirs (third/dual m/f) هذا كتابك وهذا كتابهما
ha-dha ketaa-bak wa ha-dha ketaa-bahoma
this is your book and this yours (second/dual m/f) هذا كتابكما هذا كتابك
ha-dha ketaa-bak wa ha-dha ketaa-bakoma
this is your book and this ours (first/plural) هذا كتابك وهذا كتابنا
ha-dha ketaa-bak wa ha-dha ketaa-bana
this is her book and this theirs (pl. m) هذا كتابها وهذا كتابهم
ha-dha ketaa-baha wa ha-dha ketaa-bahom
this is his book and this theirs (pl. f) هذا كتابه وهذا كتابهن
ha-dha ketaa-boh wa ha-dha ketaa-bahun-na

Verbs

Verbs are usually regular in Arabic and are formed by attaching prefixes and suffixes to the root (the basic form) of the verb. The following table outlines the prefixes and suffixes for all verbs in the present, the past (or perfect) and the imperfect tenses. You must work out what the root of the verb is and then you can modulate it with the relevant subject. As an example, below are the different forms of the verb شرب *sharaba* (to drink) conjugated with different subjects. The root in Arabic is three letters ش ر ب *sh r b*, pronounced *sharaba*. The root of a verb is typically the same as the 3rd person masculine past form: هو شرب *hu-wa sharaba* he drank. Note that all verbs in the dictionary are translated and transliterated in the 3rd person masculine. To get the infinitive and conjugate them with other subjects, you need to delete the prefix يـ *ya* and replace it with the appropriate one.

Present

In the present form, *a* should be added before the last consonant:

singular

1st person	**a**-shrab	(*ash-rab*)
2nd person m	**ta**-shrab	(*tash-rab*)
2nd person f	**ta**-shrab-**ee-na**	(*tashra-beena*)
3rd person m	**ya**-shrab	(*yash-rab*)
3rd person f	**ta**-shrab	(*tash-rab*)

dual
2nd person m	**ta**-shrab-**an**	(tash-rab-na)
2nd person f	**ta**-shrab-**an**	(tash-rab-na)
3rd person m	**ya**-shrab-**an**	(yash-rab-na)
3rd person f	**ta**-shrab-**an**	(tash-rab-na)

plural
1st person	**na**-shrab	(nash-rab)
2nd person m	**ta**-shrab-**oon**	(tashra-boon)
2nd person f	**ya**-shrab-**na**	(yash-rab-na)
3rd person m	**ya**-shrab-**oon**	(yashra-boon)
3rd person f	**ya**-shrab-**na**	(tash-rab-na)

Past (perfect)

The past or perfect tense denotes an action already completed. To form the perfect tense, the following suffixes are added to the perfect stem.

singular
1st person	sharab-**too**	(sharab-to)
2nd person m	sharab-**ta**	(sharab-ta)
2nd person f	sharab-**te**	(sharab-te)
3rd person m	sharab-**a**	(sharaba)
3rd person f	sharab-**at**	(sharabat)

dual
2nd person m	sharab-**toma**	(sharab-toma)
2nd person f	sharab-**toma**	(sharab-toma)
3rd person m	sharab-**a**	(sharaba)
3rd person f	sharab-**ata**	(sharabata)

plural
1st person	sharab-**na**	(sharab-na)
2nd person m	sharab-**tom**	(shrab-tom)
2nd person f	sharab-**tun-na**	(sharab-ton-na)
3rd person m	sharab-**oo**	(sharaboo)
3rd person f	sharab-**na**	(sharab-na)

Imperfect

Imperfect verbs describe an action in progress and must be given a suffix and a prefix to construct the proper verb form. The illustrative verb used below is يشرب *yash-rab* (to drink).

singular

1st person	**ba**-shrab (*bash-rab*)
2nd person m	**beta**-shrab (*be-tash-rab*)
2nd person f	**beta**-shrab**ee** (*be-tash-rabee*)
3rd person m	**beya**-shrab (*be-yash-rab*)
3rd person f	**beta**-shrab (*be-tash-rab*)

dual

2nd person m	**beta**-shrab**aa** (*be-tash-rabaa*)
2nd person f	**beta**-shrab**aa** (*be-tash-rabaa*)
3rd person m	**beya**-shrab**aa** (*be-yash-rabaa*)
3rd person f	**beya**-shrab**aa** (*be-yash-rabaa*)

plural

1st person	**bena**-shrab (*be-nash-rab*)
2nd person m	**beta**-shrab**oo** (*be-tash-raboo*)
2nd person f	**beta**-shrab-**na** (*be-tash-rab-na*)
3rd person m	**beya**-shrab**oo** (*be-yash-raboo*)
3rd person f	**beya**-shrab-**na** (*be-yash-rab-na*)

Negatives

To form the negative, the present form of the verb (which is already conjugated with a prefix agreeing with the subject) is preceded with one of the negative articles. The articles express the tense of the sentences:

لا *laa* indicates the negation of something as a fact or a habit, eg

انا لا ادخّن *ana laa odakh-khin* I don't smoke

لم *lam* negates a past occurrence, eg

لم أذهب إلي المتحف *lam adh-hab ila al-mat-Haf* I did not go to the museum

لن *lan* negates a future occurrence, eg

لن تذهب زوجتي إلي الطبيب غدا *lan tadh-hab zaw-jatee ila al-Tabeeb ghadan* my wife will not see the doctor tomorrow

HOLIDAYS AND FESTIVALS

NATIONAL HOLIDAYS

Administrative offices, banks and most shops are closed on these days.

7 January	**Coptic Christmas Day**
25 April	**Sinai Liberation Day**, celebrating the withdrawal of Israeli troops from the Sinai Peninsula
1 May	**Labour Day**
18 June	**Evacuation Day** (*Eid el Galaa*), commemorating the withdrawal of foreign troops from Egypt in 1954
23 July	**Revolution Day** (*El Sawra*), Egypt's national day, celebrating the 1952 revolution which ended monarchical rule in Egypt and introduced the republican regime
6 October	**Armed Forces Day**, celebrating the Egyptian army's crossing into Sinai in 1973
24 October	**Suez Day** or **Popular Resistance Day**, commemorating the ceasefire in 1973 which restored control of the Suez Canal to Egypt
2 December	**National Day** in United Arab Emirates
23 December	**Victory Day**, commemorating the war fought on Egyptian soil in 1956 between Egypt and the UK, France and Israel after the nationalization of the Suez Canal

RELIGIOUS FESTIVALS

The Islamic or **hijri** calendar is the lunar calendar used by Muslims everywhere to determine the correct dates of Islamic holy days. The calendar dates from the year the prophet Muhammad emigrated from Mecca to Medina (an event known as **Hijra**), so each numbered year is preceded by the abbreviation AH (from the Latin *anno Hegirae*). The year AH 1429 corresponds to 2008 in the Western calendar.

The Islamic calendar has 12 months in a year and is about 11 days shorter than the solar year. Islamic holy days are movable feasts, generally falling 11 days earlier each year.

All Muslim religious holidays are celebrated throughout the Arabic-speaking world, but individual countries have their own non-religious holidays.

Coptic Christmas is celebrated on the 6th and 7th of January. On the night of the 6th, Coptic Christians go to Church for a late mass. This is followed by a midnight dinner featuring turkey. On the morning of the 7th, people exchange gifts and children visit their grandparents for Christmas lunch.

Many Christians in the Middle East celebrate Christmas on 25th December, though some of the customs differ from British ones. In Lebanon, for example, families gather on Christmas Eve to have a meal together and exchange gifts. The following day may be spent with family, or socializing with friends.

The **Day of Aara-fat** is the 9th day of the Islamic month of *Dhul-Hij-ja* (the Month of Pilgrimage). It marks the culmination of the annual Islamic pilgrimage to Mecca (Saudi Arabia), known as the **Haji**. Muslim pilgrims spend the whole day from dawn till dusk praying for forgiveness. Muslims who have not made the pilgrimage often spend the day fasting and praying.

The festival of **Eid ul-Adha** marks the end of the Haji and generally lasts four days. It honours the prophet Ibrahim, who was willing to sacrifice his son if God wished it (God gave him a ram to sacrifice instead). On the first day at dawn Muslims go to the mosque to pray, and every family is meant to slaughter a sheep or goat to share with the poor and needy. Then young people visit their older relatives and families gather at the home of the oldest member for a meal. In Egypt, the traditional dish is a soup called "fata" made with lamb and bread.

Al hijra is the Muslim New Year, held on the first day of the month of Muharram to commemorate the "hijra". People generally celebrate with a family meal, and are encouraged to think about the meaning of "hijra".

Mawlid al-nabi, held in the third month of the Islamic calendar (*Rabi' al-awwal*), celebrates the birth of the prophet Muhammad. It is a festival comparable to Christmas: people decorate their homes and put on their best clothes to enjoy a special celebratory meal with family and friends. They may exchange cards and gifts, or make and distribute traditional sweets. People also gather to hear religous leaders narrate stories about the life of the Prophet.

Shamm al-Naseem ("the smell of spring") is believed to have been celebrated by Egyptians for more than 4500 years to mark the coming of spring. It is held on the spring equinox. In ancient Egypt, people would offer eggs, salted fish, lettuce and onion to the gods, and today people often enjoy these foods at picnics on the day.

Ramadan is the ninth month of the Muslim lunar calendar and the holiest month of the year. Throughout the month adult Muslims must fast from dawn till dusk, as well as abstaining from sexual activity and smoking. They may break their fast with a small meal known as the "iftar" at sunset, before going to the mosque to pray. Another meal, the "suhoor", is allowed just before sunrise. During Ramadan, Muslims are encouraged to think pure thoughts, do good deeds and generally contemplate their faith.

Eid ul-Fitr (sometimes just called **Eid**) is a three-day festival marking the end of Ramadan. It is a joyful occasion celebrating the end of the fast as well as the spiritual strength it is said to bring. It officially begins with the first sighting of the new moon. Muslims rise early to attend large public prayer ceremonies, then put on their best clothes and get together for celebratory meals. Tradition also dictates that people should give money to the poor at this time.

USEFUL ADDRESSES

In Egypt

British Embassy
7 Ahmed Ragheb Street
Garden City
Cairo
Tel: 202 794 0852
E-mail: info@britishembassy.org.eg
Website: www.britishembassy.gov.uk/egypt

American Embassy
8 Kamal El Din Salah Street
Garden City
Cairo
Tel: 202 797 3300
E-mail: consularcairo@state.gov
Website: cairo.usembassy.gov

In the United Arab Emirates

British Embassy (Dubai)
Al Seef Street
PO Box 65
Tel: 971 4 309 4444
E-mail: consular.dubai@fco.gov.uk
Website: www.britishembassy.gov.uk/uae

British Embassy (Abu Dhabi)
22 Khalid bin Al Waleed Street
PO Box 248
Tel: 971 2 610 1100
E-mail: consularenquiries.ad@fco.gov.uk
Website: www.britishembassy.gov.uk/uae

US Consulate (Dubai)
21st floor
Dubai World Trade Center
PO Box 9343
Dubai
Tel: 971 4 311 6000
E-mail: dubaiwarden@state.gov.
Website: http://dubai.usconsulate.gov.

US Embassy (Abu Dhabi)
Embassies District
Plot 38
Sector W59-02
Street No 4
Abu Dhabi
Tel: 971 2 414 2200; (after hours) 971 2 414 2500
E-mail: consularabudha@state.gov.
Website: http://uae.usembassy.gov/

In the UK
Egyptian Embassy
2 Lowndes Street
London
SW1 9ET
Tel: 020 7235 9777
E-mail: info@egyptianconsulate.co.uk
Website: www.egyptianconsulate.co.uk

United Arab Emirates Embassy
30 Princes Gate
London
SW7 1PT
Tel: 0207 581 1281; (consular section) 0207 808 8302
E-mail: information@uaeembassyuk.net
Website: www.uaeembassyuk.net

Egyptian Tourism Office
Tel: 0207 493 5283
Website: tourismegypt@visitegypt.org.uk

In the US
Egyptian Embassy
3521 International CTM.W.
Washington DC, 20008
Tel: 202 895 5400
E-mail: embassy@egyptembdc.org
Website: http://www.egyptembassy.us

Egyptian Consulate
1110 Second Avenue
New York 10022
Tel: 212 759 7120/7121/7122
E-mail: info@egyptnyc.net
Website: http://www.egyptnyc.net/

Embassy of the United Arab Emirates
3522 International Court
NW Washington DC 20008
Tel: 202 363 3009; (cultural division) 202 243 4444; (New York) 212 371 0480
Website: www.uae-embassy.org

CONVERSION TABLES

Note that when writing numbers, Arabic uses a comma where English uses a full stop. For example, 0.6 would be written 0,6 in Arabic and pronounced as *sitta min 'ashra*.

MEASUREMENTS

Only the metric system is used in Arabic-speaking countries.

Length
1 cm ≈ 0.4 inches
30 cm ≈ 1 foot

Distance
1 metre ≈ 1 yard
1 km ≈ 0.6 miles

To convert kilometres into miles, divide by 8 and then multiply by 5.

kilometres	1	2	5	10	20	100
miles	0.6	1.25	3.1	6.25	12.50	62.5

To convert miles into kilometres, divide by 5 and then multiply by 8.

miles	1	2	5	10	20	100
kilometres	1.6	3.2	8	16	32	160

Weight
25g ≈ 1 oz   1 kg ≈ 2 lb   6 kg ≈ 1 stone

To convert kilos into pounds, divide by 5 and then multiply by 11.
To convert pounds into kilos, multiply by 5 and then divide by 11.

kilos	1	2	10	20	60	80
pounds	2.2	4.4	22	44	132	176

Liquid
1 litre ≈ 2 pints
4.5 litres ≈ 1 gallon

Temperature

To convert temperatures in Fahrenheit into Celsius, subtract 32, multiply by 5 and then divide by 9.

To convert temperatures in Celsius into Fahrenheit, divide by 5, multiply by 9 and then add 32.

Fahrenheit (°F)	32	40	50	59	68	86	100
Celsius (°C)	0	4	10	15	20	30	38

Clothes sizes

Sometimes you will find sizes given using the English-language abbreviations **XS** (Extra Small), **S** (Small), **M** (Medium), **L** (Large) and **XL** (Extra Large).

- **Women's clothes**

Arabic countries	36	38	40	42	44	etc
UK	8	10	12	14	16	

- **Bras (cup sizes are the same)**

Arabic countries	70	75	80	85	90	etc
UK	32	34	36	38	40	

- **Men's shirts (collar size)**

Arabic countries	36	38	41	43	etc
UK	14	15	16	17	

- **Men's clothes**

Arabic countries	40	42	44	46	48	50	etc
UK	30	32	34	36	38	40	

- **Women's shoes**

Arabic countries	37	38	39	40	42	etc
UK	4	5	6	7	8	

- **Men's shoes**

Arabic countries	40	42	43	44	46	etc
UK	7	8	9	10	11	